The Old Regime and the Revolution

The Old Regime and the Revolution

Trevor Cairns

Published in cooperation with Cambridge University Press
Lerner Publications Company, Minneapolis

LIBRARY OF CONGRESS CATALOGING IN PUBLICATION DATA

Cairns, Trevor.
The old regime and the revolution.

(The Cambridge Introduction to History, v. 7)
1. Europe — History — 18th century — Juvenile literature.
2. France — History — Revolution, 1789-1799 — Juvenile literature. 3. History, Modern — 18th century — Juvenile literature.
I. Title.

D286.C3 1980   940.2'53   79-2972
ISBN 0-8225-0807-9

This edition first published 1980 by Lerner Publications Company
by permission of Cambridge University Press.

International Standard Book Number: 0-8225-0807-9
Library of Congress Catalog Card Number: 79-2972

Manufactured in the United States of America.

This edition is available exclusively from:
Lerner Publications Company, 241 First Avenue North, Minneapolis, Minnesota 55401

1 2 3 4 5 6 7 8 9 10 85 84 83 82 81 80

Contents

List of Maps and Diagrams

Editors' Note

In preparing this edition of *The Cambridge Introduction to History* for publication, the editors have made only a few minor changes in the original material. In some isolated cases, British spelling and usage were altered in order to avoid possible confusion for our readers. Whenever necessary, information was added to clarify references to people, places, and events in British history. An index and a list of maps and diagrams were also provided in each volume.

All references to money in this book are given in British monetary units. The basic unit is the pound (£), which is equal to 20 shillings (s) or 100 pence (d). In recent years, the value of the British pound has varied from about $2.50 to about $1.50 in U.S. currency.

The Emperor Napoleon in his coronation robes

Louis XIV; born 1638, king 1643, began to rule personally 1661, died 1715. This life-sized portrait by H. Rigaud, painted in 1701, shows the king in his robes of state at the age of sixty-three. Louis commissioned the painting as a gift for his grandson who was claiming the Spanish throne, but he liked it so much that he kept it, and had a copy made to be sent to Spain.

1 THE POLITICS OF KINGS

Royal zenith

The court of the Grand Monarch

This is Louis XIV of France.

What impression does he make? Majestic? Magnificent? Glorious, even? That is what he intended, certainly. He had accepted from flattering subjects the title of 'the Great', and took as his badge the sun itself. In French he is known as 'le grand monarque' and his lifetime is 'le grand siècle' – the great monarch and the great century.

Next you see his bedroom in the palace of Versailles. He retired and rose with ceremony. Privileged courtiers waited in the room, the very favoured stood within the rail, and the most highly honoured of all were permitted to help the king to dress and undress. The greatest nobles in France acted as valets to the Sun King.

The bedchamber of Louis XIV is in the very centre of the east front of the palace of Versailles, so that the windows overlook the great court and admit the morning sun. This photograph is taken from where the royal bed stood, draped in gold-embroidered crimson velvet, and shows the richness of the setting in which the king placed himself. Beyond the rail the more public part of the room forms a passageway between the king's salon, or drawing-room, and his council-chamber.

The entire palace was designed to provide a suitable setting for his glittering court. Mirrors reflected countless candles in crystal chandeliers, gilded furnishings, rich costumes. Paintings recorded the victories of the king's armies. Outside it was just as impressive. On one front the enormous courtyard contained a single statue of the king. From the other front extended the gardens and park, laid out in classic dignity with avenues, statues and fountains.

Louis created Versailles deliberately. Once, when he was a child, rioters had burst into his bedroom in the old royal palace in Paris. Versailles was far enough out of the capital to be safe from sudden affronts, yet near enough for messages to pass quickly. The splendid show, too, had a solid reason behind it. Louis knew how people judged by appearances. If he looked like the most magnificent king in Europe, it would help him really to become so.

It was his policy to attract the nobles to Versailles. Only a few years before, turbulent nobles had plotted and stirred up

riots. At court he could keep a close watch on them. They could be led to compete for royal favours, to rival each other in extravagance, in fine fashionable clothes, jewellery, in reckless gambling. Some nobles understood and resented what was happening to them, but nobody who wanted to be regarded as important could afford to stay away from court. For Louis was able to build up a belief that everything happened at Versailles, nothing anywhere else. A nobleman ordered to retire to his estates was not only disgraced, he was exiled from all that made life worth living.

In truth, was life at court so very marvellous? Louis hired the finest entertainers. There were masques with music by Lully, there were the latest comedies by Molière. There were paintings to admire by Lebrun and Mignard, sculptures by Girardon. But what was there to *do*? Some courtiers were sent as ambassadors to foreign courts, or given commands in the army or navy – though some of these spent more time at court than at their posts. For the rest, when the ceremonies and amusements were over, they could gossip, or try to be noticed by the king, or quarrel. The palace was overcrowded and uncomfortable, and cleanliness was difficult. But perfume was used freely, and everything was gilded.

Versailles was a splendid success. The court dazzled not only France, but the whole of Europe.

left: *The palace of Versailles, painted by D. Martin in 1722. This shows the courtyard front, but there is also a glimpse of the park beyond.*

above: *A scene from the opera* The Festivals of Love and of Bacchus, *written by the king's favourite composer, J. B. Lully, and performed in the open-air theatre at Versailles in 1674. The engraving was published in 1678.*

above: *'The Rape of Proserpine', one of the classical sculptures by F. Girardon which stands in the gardens of Versailles.*

A portrait in the style of P. Mignard showing Madame de Montespan, one of the king's mistresses, posed with her children.

Sources of strength

Louis XIV had to pay a price. He had to lead his entire life in public. Everything he did was watched and talked about. Even when he did snatch a few hours' privacy his courtiers would be guessing and gossiping. Doubtless all princes were born to a public life and accepted it, but the Sun King's performance had to be something special.

He worked hard at creating an overwhelming image, and also at governing France. Every day he spent hours with his advisers and secretaries, listening, discussing, deciding. No matter how good his ministers were, the final responsibility must be the king's; otherwise he would not have been master.

Louis obviously spent vast sums of money, and one of the main problems of his ministers was how to get it. Between 1662 and 1683 Jean Baptiste Colbert was minister of finance. He was clear-headed, hard-working and highly efficient.

His first task was to ensure that the taxes did reach the government, for much was being wasted and pilfered. Colbert abolished unnecessary jobs and insisted on strict new methods of book-keeping and accounting. A special tribunal was busy for four years prosecuting people who had swindled the government. Another difficulty was tax-farming, the system by which the government sold to a businessman the right to collect the taxes in a certain district for a fixed number of years. This saved the government the trouble of collecting, but obviously the tax-farmer was making a profit and therefore the government must be getting less than it ought. Colbert did not end this system, but he made the tax-farmers pay more; by all-round strictness he greatly increased the yield of the taxes without making any sweeping changes in the system.

Gold was 'the sinews of war', and Colbert wanted as much as he could get. France was the largest and most fertile kingdom in Europe, with large population, food, raw materials like wood and iron; but no goldmines. Gold must come from trade, through selling more and buying less. Therefore Colbert tried to build up industries: wool, silk, tapestry, lace, glass. Many of the products were luxury articles for which wealthy customers might pay high prices. He invited foreign workmen to settle in France. He framed regulations about the quality of French manufactures. He improved roads and waterways. The Languedoc Canal, completed in 1681, was the first great canal in Europe, at least since Roman times, and bore goods from the Atlantic to the Mediterranean coast without the long and sometimes dangerous voyage round Spain.

There was wealth across the oceans, too. Other nations, the Portuguese and Spanish, then the Dutch and the English, had long since founded their empires and trading companies. French enterprise seemed feeble in comparison, but Colbert would do his best, as the map opposite shows, to carve a share for France. And that involved building a strong navy.

So Colbert worked to make France prosper; not so that the people would be happy, but so that the state would be strong. (What does 'the state' mean? Louis XIV is said to have declared, 'I am the state'.)

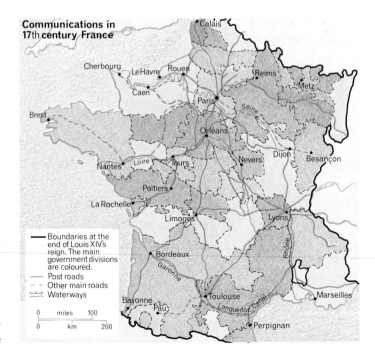

Communications in 17th century France

Calais
Cherbourg
Le Havre   Rouen   Reims
Caen   Metz
Brest   Paris
Seine
Orléans
Nantes   Loire   Tours   Nevers   Dijon   Besançon
Poitiers
La Rochelle
Limoges   Lyons
Bordeaux   Rhône
Garonne
Bayonne   Toulouse   Marseilles
Pau   Languedoc Canal
Perpignan

— Boundaries at the end of Louis XIV's reign. The main government divisions are coloured.
— Post roads
--- Other main roads
≕ Waterways

0   miles   100
0   km   200

Though he achieved much, Colbert was not completely successful. The colony of Canada remained small because so few people wanted to settle there. The French East India Company fell badly into debt, and so did the West India Company, though similar companies belonging to other nations made money. Was this because Frenchmen were such poor merchants that they could not manage even with government help? Or was it government interference that damped down the boldness and ambition which successful pioneers needed?

In 1685, two years after Colbert's death, the king's religious policy may have harmed trade. The Religious Wars had ended long ago, and by the Edict of Nantes in 1598 the Huguenots (French Protestants) had been allowed to worship in their own way. Although France was a Catholic country, the French government, even when directed by cardinals, had usually put politics before religion; never hesitating, for instance, to help Protestants or even Muslims against the Catholic powers of Spain and Austria. In the 1620s Cardinal Richelieu had deprived the Huguenots of their military strongholds, but only so that they could not be a danger to the state: he had not interfered with their freedom of religion. But Louis decided that his subjects must all accept his Catholic beliefs, revoked the Edict of Nantes and ordered a severe persecution of Huguenots. Many of them escaped abroad, and they included excellent merchants and craftsmen. The English silk industry, to take only one example, was begun by Huguenot refugees. There was no sudden slump, but obviously what France lost, many other countries, some of them enemies, gained.

Despite these setbacks Colbert's work made France capable of paying for the Grand Monarch. It was this need for money, for taxable wealth, that caused Colbert to build up prosperity in France, and ironically it was this same need that eventually bled the prosperity away. For the time came when the king demanded more than his country could afford. It was not Versailles, expensive though that was, which soaked up French wealth, but the most costly royal occupation of all: war.

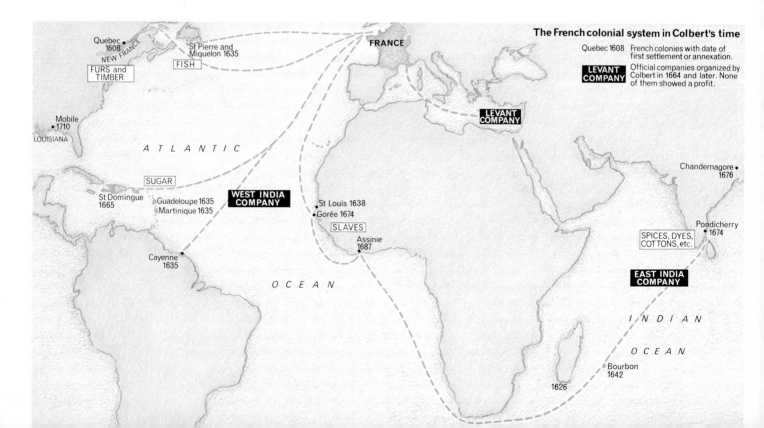

The French colonial system in Colbert's time

Quebec 1608 French colonies with date of first settlement or annexation.

LEVANT COMPANY Official companies organized by Colbert in 1664 and later. None of them showed a profit.

A contemporary French print showing the capture of
Mons in 1691 by Louis XIV in person. The royal party is
in the foreground. Beyond lies the city, protected by
medieval walls and more up-to-date geometrical defences.
The attackers have constructed trenches, drainage ditches
and batteries.

The pursuit of greatness

Louis XIV meant to be 'Great'. Several rulers from earlier ages
are known by that title, men like Pope Gregory or King Alfred
or Emperor Otto, and later in this book you will learn of others.
What does 'the Great' mean? Can it mean many different
things?

The picture shows what 'greatness' meant to Louis XIV. The map shows the score in terms of territory.

Louis prided himself on always being in the right. He may honestly have believed this, but in practice it looked more like always having some plausible legal excuse for taking what he wanted. His first war, in 1667, was an invasion of lands which, he claimed, his Spanish wife ought to have inherited. During the 1680s, in time of peace, he sent troops into parts of Alsace which he claimed under various treaties, and set up courts to examine his claims; his courts decided in his favour.

Right or wrong, it was not the arguments of his lawyers which gained lands for Louis, but the strength and skill of his soldiers. He had the best army in Europe, and some excellent generals. Perhaps the most important was an engineer, Vauban. Warfare in the late seventeenth century had become a slow business because fortifications were so strong and numerous, especially in the Low Countries. There were far more sieges than pitched battles, and siegecraft was now so mathematical that good engineers could predict how long a siege should last. Though uncomfortable and deadly for the men in the trenches, this form of warfare was ideal for stately inspections by royal visitors, and ceremonial entries into surrendered cities.

Behind the dignity, however, war still meant treachery, hatred and cruelty. In 1672 Louis attacked the Dutch (whom he called 'maggots') without declaring war. The Dutch defended themselves with the same fierce determination they had once shown against the Spaniards, and chose another Prince William of Orange to lead them. He swore he would fight to the last ditch, and there he would die. It never came to that because the Dutch flooded their countryside, and Louis XIV's army came to a halt in the mud. During that same war the French general Turenne deliberately tried to reduce the fertile Palatinate into a lifeless desert. Louis himself had no part in the destruction and slaughter, but there were many people, especially in Germany, who would not forget that the misery and death were part of the Sun King's glory.

By the 1680s Louis seemed to have achieved his ambition. In art and fashion, politics and war Versailles gave the lead to all Europe. But success can raise up enemies. Every gain had been at the expense of someone else. He was admired, but also envied and feared. By now there were many who wished to see his power brought low.

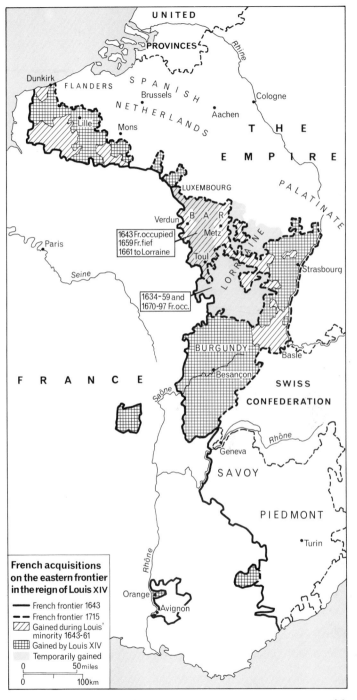

1643 Fr. occupied
1659 Fr. fief
1661 to Lorraine

1634–59 and
1670–97 Fr. occ.

**French acquisitions
on the eastern frontier
in the reign of Louis XIV**

—— French frontier 1643
– – French frontier 1715
▨ Gained during Louis' minority 1643–61
▦ Gained by Louis XIV
Temporarily gained

0   50 miles
0   100 km

Europe c. 1690

Population estimates in millions

	0	5	10	15	20
France					
Spain					
Portugal					
Eng.&Wales					
Scotland					
Ireland					
United Prov.					
The Empire					
Habsburg L.					
SwissConfed.					
Sweden					
Denmark					
Milan					
Venice					
Tuscany					
Naples					
Poland					

The Balance of Power

The states of western Europe formed an association, a sort of league. The rules and the relative positions of the members were not written down, but every statesman understood them. This was the system of international politics and diplomacy which had grown up about the time of the Renaissance and now seemed thoroughly normal and natural.

There were FIVE BIG POWERS. First came FRANCE. Next were two states ruled by members of the Habsburg family, rivals of the French kings for nearly two centuries. AUSTRIA was fairly strong, though her ruler, the Emperor, had very little authority over the other German states which made up what was still called the Holy Roman Empire. SPAIN, though still in control of most of Italy and an enormous colonial empire, was bankrupt, exhausted, her king a sickly near-imbecile. The other two powers were the UNITED PROVINCES (of the Netherlands) and BRITAIN. Both depended mainly on trade and shipping for their wealth and strength but, though primarily naval powers, they could raise or hire formidable armies.

SWEDEN was respected. Though neither numerous nor rich,

the Swedes had been looked upon as the great warriors of the north since the victories of Gustavus Adolphus in the Thirty Years' War. Sweden held key positions all round the Baltic Sea, and this was an area very important to other parts of Europe for its grain, timber, flax and hemp, tar and iron; some of these, classed as 'naval stores,' were vital to any state with a big navy. Nevertheless, north-eastern Europe remained mostly on the fringe of European big-power politics, and had its own system of alliances and enmities, treaties and wars; only at times did these affairs get entangled with the main European international affairs.

There were also several smaller states, mainly German, which would line up beside the bigger powers. Their soldiers were sometimes useful, and the prince of a small state might pick up good rewards in the peace treaty if his men had done well in the war.

These governments were the players in a power game. Each tried to gain and to prevent his neighbours from gaining. Yesterday's enemy could be today's ally — and tomorrow an enemy again; everybody accepted the fact that situations changed. But there were some principles that did not change, and the main one was this: *no single power must be allowed to become strong enough to overwhelm the rest.*

This common-sense rule was not a new discovery, but, under the name of the Balance of Power, it was being recognized as *the* great law of international politics. Now it was about to work against Louis XIV.

In the war which lasted from 1688 to 1697 Louis found himself opposed by all four of the other big powers, besides some smaller ones. In spite of this the French armies did well, but Louis gained nothing at the peace treaty.

The last and greatest of Louis XIV's wars is called the War of the Spanish Succession. It was, indeed, about who should succeed to the Spanish throne. The diplomatic details are complicated, but the main position is simple enough. There were two strong claims: the Austrian Habsburgs and the family of Louis XIV. Representatives of some of the chief powers met, and eventually Louis signed a treaty embodying the arrangement shown in the first map, by which his son received far less than the Emperor's. But the Emperor did not agree — he thought that his family should get even more.

There was one party that had not been consulted — the government of Spain itself. The dying king of Spain understood

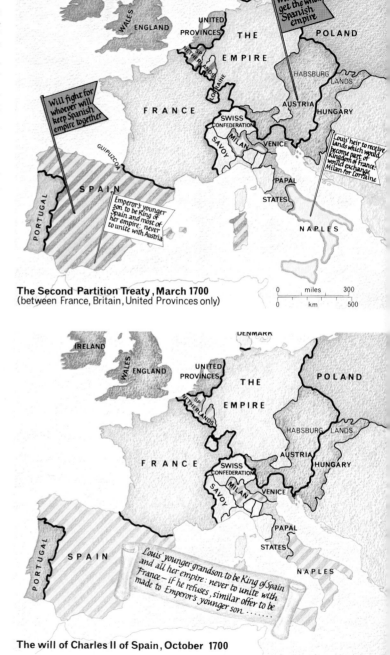

The Second Partition Treaty, March 1700
(between France, Britain, United Provinces only)

0 miles 300
0 km 500

The will of Charles II of Spain, October 1700

13

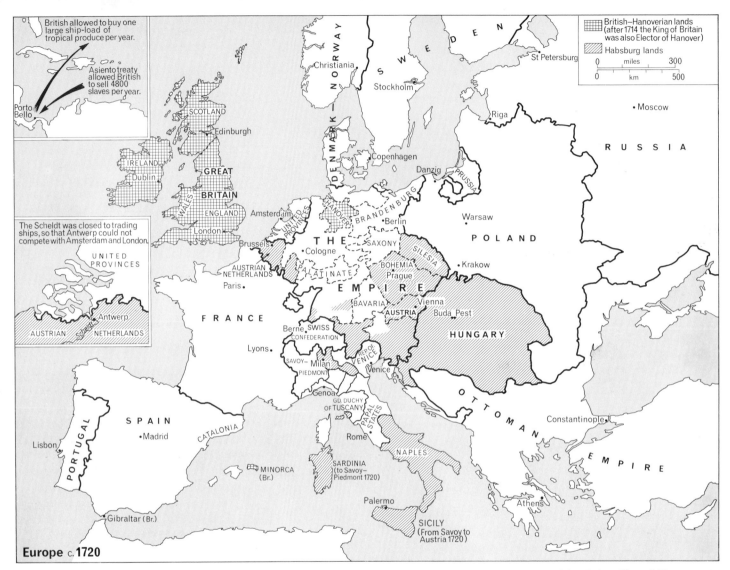

British allowed to buy one large ship-load of tropical produce per year.

Asiento treaty allowed British to sell 4800 slaves per year.

Porto Bello

The Scheldt was closed to trading ships, so that Antwerp could not compete with Amsterdam and London.

UNITED PROVINCES

Antwerp
Scheldt
AUSTRIAN NETHERLANDS

British–Hanoverian lands (after 1714 the King of Britain was also Elector of Hanover)

Habsburg lands

0 miles 300
0 km 500

Christiania
Stockholm
St Petersburg
Moscow
Riga
Copenhagen
Danzig
Berlin
Warsaw
Krakow
SCOTLAND
Edinburgh
IRELAND
Dublin
GREAT BRITAIN
WALES
ENGLAND
London
Amsterdam
Brussels
UNITED PROVINCES
HANOVER
BRANDENBURG
PRUSSIA
RUSSIA
POLAND
SWEDEN
DENMARK–NORWAY
AUSTRIAN NETHERLANDS
Paris
Cologne
THE EMPIRE
SAXONY
SILESIA
BOHEMIA
Prague
PALATINATE
BAVARIA
Vienna
AUSTRIA
Buda Pest
HUNGARY
FRANCE
Berne SWISS CONFEDERATION
Lyons
SAVOY
Milan
PIEDMONT
REP. OF VENICE
Venice
Genoa
GD. DUCHY OF TUSCANY
PAPAL STATES
Rome
OTTOMAN EMPIRE
Constantinople
PORTUGAL
Lisbon
SPAIN
Madrid
CATALONIA
MINORCA (Br.)
SARDINIA (to Savoy–Piedmont 1720)
NAPLES
Palermo
Athens
Gibraltar (Br.)
SICILY (From Savoy to Austria 1720)

Europe c. 1720

enough to resent any attempt to divide his possessions, and many Spaniards were furious that foreigners should dare to divide up their empire. The result was that the king made a will, leaving everything to a younger grandson of Louis XIV.

The two maps on the previous page show the choice before Louis. He chose to accept the will.

In the war that followed in 1702 France was supported against the other powers by most of Spain. But this time the best generals were on the other side. John Churchill, created Duke of Marlborough for his victories, commanded the British and Dutch forces in the Low Countries. Prince Eugene was the outstanding Austrian commander. By 1709 Marlborough was pushing out of the Low Countries into France. Marlborough wanted to march on Paris. It seemed possible that the Grand Monarch was going to lose all that he had spent his life acquiring.

Louis was saved by a number of things. His soldiers — not the generals, but the ordinary Frenchmen in the ranks — began to fight with a new determination now that France itself was threatened. In England the Whig Party, which wanted to smash Louis XIV, lost the favour of Queen Anne, and the Tories, who were not at all keen on the war, took over the government. But what made it certain that Louis would survive was the Balance of Power. It tipped in his favour.

What tilted the Balance was this: the Austrian prince whom the Allies wanted to place on the Spanish throne became Emperor in 1711, as the result of unexpected deaths in the Habsburg family. But he insisted on keeping both Austrian and Spanish thrones himself. This would mean something very much like a revival of the empire of Charles V, and most statesmen thought it would make him far too powerful. (Charles was his name too: Charles VI.) Louis was at least ready to promise that if the French prince became King of Spain, his branch of the royal family would be cut out of the French succession. The two crowns of France and Spain would never be united. Perhaps Louis was now a lesser danger than the Emperor?

Therefore Britain secretly came to an understanding with France, and most of the Allies then agreed to peace terms at Utrecht in 1713. Austria tried to fight alone, but was not strong enough. So there was a general peace in 1714, though it was 1725 before the Emperor could being himself to sign a treaty with the new king of Spain.

The Balance of Power had started the war, and the Balance of Power ended it.

Louis XIV died in 1715. He had done more than any man of his times to shape the new century. In politics, the map of western Europe, or the system of alliances and balances with France as the leading power, was mainly the result of his ambitions and wars. Within France he had set an example of complete royal authority which other kings envied; the eighteenth century was to be the great age of despotic monarchs. Important though all this was, the influence of France may have been even deeper in other things. The fashions, the manners, the whole elegant culture of eighteenth-century life among the upper classes reflected the example of Versailles and Paris. French became the international language of polite society. The Sun King may not have planned just this, but he stamped an image on the future of Europe.

As for the people who did not belong to polite society, the

Huguenot refugees, part of a contemporary Dutch engraving. Propaganda prints like this helped to convince ordinary people that the politics of their princes were important to them too.

people who, in every country in Europe, paid the taxes of the government and the rents of the landowners, filled the ranks of the army, and regarded poverty and hardship as commonplace facts of life; what did they think of the politics of kings? It is easy to conclude that it was no more than a vast power game in which the ordinary people had no genuine interest but for which they paid in money and in blood. The ordinary people of Paris rejoiced when Louis XIV died. But remember the Dutch flooding their land to stop Louis, the Germans who hated the destroyers of the Palatinate, the French who fought differently when their own land was in danger. In Spain the people rose and fought for the king of their choice – most for the Bourbon prince, but the Catalans for the Habsburg. In England and Scotland most people probably thought of Louis XIV as a Catholic tyrant who would try to put the exiled Stuarts back on the British throne – and that would mean Catholic tyranny in Britain. All these people, and more, must have thought, rightly or wrongly, that the wars were their business as well as the king's.

The eighteenth century was to be full of wars between the European powers, and many of them sound, from their titles, as though they were nothing more than squabbles between royal families about who should inherit what – after the Spanish Succession came Polish, Austrian, Bavarian Succession wars. And the others, on the whole, look very much the same: land-grabs and deals. Was this the whole truth? Who – if anyone – was better off at the end of it?

Two new powers

Quite early in the century statesmen became aware that the stage had become wider. The big powers now had to recognize two new members of their group, both in north-eastern Europe.

Brandenburg becomes Prussia

The north-east corner of the Holy Roman Empire was the Electorate of Brandenburg. It was a frontier province in the Middle Ages, the poorest and least fertile of the electorates. Since 1415 it had been ruled by the Hohenzollern family. East of Brandenburg lay Prussia, where the Order of Teutonic Knights had conquered the heathen natives, converted them to Christianity, and gone on ruling them. At the time of the Reformation the Grand Master of the Teutonic Knights was a Hohenzollern; he became a Protestant but held on to the Order's lands and eventually Prussia was added to Brandenburg. So the state began to grow, but it was still small and obscure.

Elector Frederick William, called 'the Great Elector', who reigned from 1640 to 1688, set about making his state strong and important. He tried, like Colbert in France, to increase wealth. He had more success than Colbert, perhaps because it was easier to oversee a smaller state, perhaps because he was himself the master and not merely a minister, perhaps because he spent less. He welcomed some of the hard-working Huguenots whom Louis XIV persecuted. Greatness among rulers was usually measured in territories and victories. The Great Elector added to his lands by being on the winning side at the end of the Thirty Years' War in 1648. In 1679 he fought the mighty Swedes, and at the battle of Fehrbellin he beat those champions. Among the states around the Baltic, Brandenburg was now a force to be reckoned with.

For rulers who aspired to be recognized as important throughout Europe as a whole, the title of Elector was not satisfactory; it showed that there was somebody above them. In 1701 the next Elector, with the consent of the Emperor who needed support, assumed a new title. He crowned himself King Frederick I of Prussia.

The second king, Frederick William I, who reigned from

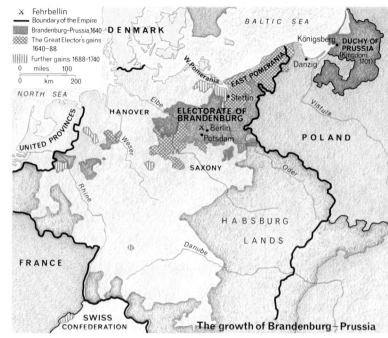

X Fehrbellin
— Boundary of the Empire
▓ Brandenburg-Prussia, 1640
▨ The Great Elector's gains 1640–88
▥ Further gains 1688–1740

0   miles   100
0   km   200

The growth of Brandenburg–Prussia

1713 to 1740, has been described as a drill sergeant. The map shows how his kingdom sprawled, with no good river or mountain frontiers to deter an invader, so it is possible to argue that Brandenburg–Prussia had to be a military state in order to survive. But that does not explain the way Frederick William behaved. He was short-tempered, violent, contemptuous of culture. He was also rigidly just and deeply concerned to protect Christianity (as he understood it); he improved elementary education among the ordinary people, and managed his land so well that he paid off his father's debts and left a full treasury to his son. He loved his army. His special pride and joy was a regiment of very tall grenadiers whom his agents recruited all over Europe; on parade, with their high grenadier caps, they looked like a regiment of giants. The army was disciplined to mechanical perfection on the parade ground, but was never tested in war. Perhaps Frederick William was not greedy for his neighbours' lands, perhaps he was a coward as well as a bully, perhaps he did not want to have his soldiers damaged. Some critics believed that his army was only fit for show, and that if it ever went on campaign the soldiers would take the chance to desert, to escape from the iron discipline.

Frederick William died exactly one hundred years after the

Great Elector began his reign. Each of the three rulers in that century had left his mark on the state. Had Prussia grown up to being a big power, or was it like a fish that seemed big in a small pond trying to look big in a large pond? The new king, Frederick II, would give the answer.

Muscovy and All the Russias

Eastwards from Prussia the north European plain broadens until it becomes a huge flat expanse stretching from the White Sea in the north to the Black Sea in the south. The vegetation gradually changes from barren tundra, to pine forests, to larch forests, to open grasslands. Some of the land was rich for agriculture, or stock-raising, or forestry. Great rivers made water transport easy. Unhappily for the Slav peoples who dwelt there, the whole area lay open to invaders.

The Vikings who travelled down the rivers in the ninth century probably did more good than harm. Their trading settlements grew to cities; Kiev on the Dnieper is sometimes classed as the first Russian kingdom, and the very name Rus refers to the Swedish settlers. They brought about contact between their neighbours and Constantinople, and so the various 'Russian' peoples became Christian according to the Byzantine or Orthodox Church. They learned to write in the Cyrillic script, not the Latin. Their paintings had the stiff unworldly look of the Byzantine icons from which they were copied. If the kingdoms of western Europe were heirs of Rome, the principalities of Russia were heirs of Byzantium. When at last the Byzantine Emperors were no more, in the fifteenth century, the Princes of Moscow claimed the title of Caesar – Czar or Tsar.

Meanwhile there had been other invaders, who seem to have done nothing but harm. In the thirteenth century Jenghis Khan's Mongols swept across eastern Europe. The Tartars of the Golden Horde finally settled to the south-east of the Russians; from Sarai they exacted tribute, with fire and sword. For many generations of terror and destruction the Russian peasants and townsmen learned to endure, patiently and courageously, and to trust for comfort to their Church, while their leaders learned to act with cunning and ruthlessness. They could not otherwise have survived.

There was no help for the Russians from the west. The Poles and Lithuanians, who about 1400 established a kingdom

The growth of Russia

stretching from the Baltic to the Black Sea, were Christians according to the Catholic Church, and drew their culture from the west and from Rome. Poles and Russians became traditional enemies. The Teutonic Knights were just as hostile, while the German Hanseatic merchants were interested only in protecting their sea-borne trade.

So Russia was left to struggle on and develop in its own way. During the fifteenth and sixteenth centuries the Tsars of Moscow managed to win lands from the Tartars and to become rulers of other Russian states until they could with some reason claim to be Tsars not only of Muscovy, but of All the Russias. They ruled over a vast empire – but vaguely defined and loosely held on the whole. Only in the west were the frontiers reasonably clear; elsewhere the empire shaded away among the forests and steppes. South and east lived the Cossacks, bold frontiersmen who obeyed the Tsar if they felt like it and who raided and probed and founded outposts far beyond the limits of settled Russian life. There were scattered little

left: *Old Russia, as shown in an illustration in a 1719 edition of a mid-seventeenth-century account. It is Palm Sunday, in front of the Kremlin.*

right: *Peter I; born 1672, joint Tsar 1682, sole Tsar 1689, died 1725. Bust by B. Rastrelli.*

groups of hunters, trappers and traders across the vastness of Siberia, even to the edge of the China Sea by the middle of the seventeenth century. To anyone in western Europe who ever bothered to think about it, Russia's future must have seemed turned towards the east.

A few westerners knew Russia, most of them merchants or soldiers of fortune adventuring in a backward empire, old-fashioned and outlandish. The skyline of Moscow, with the onion-spires of its churches, seemed weirdly oriental. The people, with their flowing garb, their furs and thick beards, did not look as though they belonged either to Europe or to the seventeenth century. The army was ill-equipped, ignorant of discipline and military science as these things were understood in the west. There were few industries and no seaports, except for Archangel which was remote and frozen up for most of the year. Yet why should the Russians want to change? They had their Church, life was no harder than it had been, and they knew of nothing better.

Some of the Tsars in the seventeenth century tried to strengthen their empire, mainly by importing modern weapons, starting iron foundries and inviting foreign workmen to settle in Russia. But things happened very slowly, and this was not only because of the endless distances. Government officials were few and weak, the local nobles powerful – indeed, contrary to the way things were moving in western Europe, the nobles had succeeded in making serfdom stricter than ever in Russia. The Tsar's ministers themselves were sometimes paralysed by rivalries and corruption. Altogether, attempts at 'modernization' were too few and feeble to make much difference to old Russia.

Peter the Great

It hardly seemed humanly possible to budge the gigantic bulk of Russia, and that may be why the Tsar who did it seems to have had a savage strength that would have fitted a great beast rather than a man. Tsar Peter I used his furious energy with iron determination and practical sense.

As a boy, Peter played soldiers. But he formed the other boys into proper military units, and sought the advice of a professional, a Swiss soldier of fortune. Peter soon came to understand how quaintly comical Russia and her army must seem to western statesmen and soldiers. He resolved to change this. He would be ruler of a first-class power, and nothing would be allowed to stand in the way.

In 1689 his effective reign as Tsar began. As soon as he felt that things were settled he did something that no earlier Tsar would even have considered. He left Russia in order to learn for himself how things were done in other lands. He chose the United Provinces and England particularly, because there he could learn most about ships. Ships – for a landlocked empire like Russia! Peter was not mad. He had decided that Russia would not remain landlocked. Only by sea could he reach out to the rest of the world, and he would make Russia a sea-power. There were also the great rivers flowing towards the Black Sea and the Caspian. So Peter studied ship-building, and to his way of thinking that meant working like an ordinary carpenter in the shipyards.

He was recalled to Russia because of a plot against him, involving the royal guards. He punished the plotters ferociously. Then he began his real work.

The map shows his conquests. They were not won easily, and Peter was unable to hold the port of Azov against the Turks. In the west his adversary was the Swedish king, Charles XII, a young man who had won the reputation of being a daring and brilliant general, and who soundly beat Peter. But Peter fought on, Charles led his army deep into Russia, and at Poltava in 1709 the Swedes suffered complete disaster. This was the decisive moment, though the statesmen of most of Europe were too involved with the Spanish Succession War to appreciate it fully. Sweden never really regained her military strength, Peter was able to occupy the Baltic coast which he so coveted and he kept it when at last peace was signed in 1721.

The map also shows how Peter tried to strengthen Russia by encouraging industries. Some of this work was directed by foreigners, some by Russians who had been abroad. Peter tried to force everything and everyone into the service of the Russian state. Nobles must not only remain wealthy landlords and serfowners. They were ordered to become officers in the army, the navy or the civil service. This might also keep them more under the eye of the government. Even the Church had to submit. The Patriarch tried to oppose some of the Tsar's actions, and was simply disregarded. When he died, Peter did not appoint a new Patriarch, but eventually set up a government department to administer the Church. Everywhere the Tsar was constantly trying to make things work better, dividing up the empire into a new system of districts, rearranging his ministers in new councils.

Peter, like Louis XIV, believed that appearances mattered. Most people have heard how he tried to force his subjects to look European by shaving off their beards. He had to have a capital fit for Europe. Moscow was quite useless. So there was built a new city, Peter's 'window on the world'. It was in the monumental classical style of western Europe. Not even the name was Russian: St Petersburg. Nobles were ordered to build mansions along the broad streets. It was intended to be the most stately capital in Europe, and so it was. The achieve-

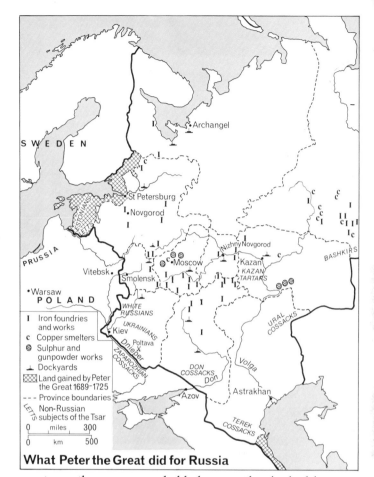

What Peter the Great did for Russia

ment was the more remarkable because the site had been an unhealthy marsh. It cost the lives of thousands of the workmen, but Peter was willing to pay the price of greatness.

Peter I spared neither himself nor others. He is said to have let his only son be flogged to death when he opposed Peter's violent reforms, though he had promised not to harm the prince. Peter cared little for truth or mercy, religion or culture, or for the happiness of his people. Within about thirty years he drove Russia into modern Europe, and it was a stupendous achievement. But it has often been argued that the changes were too quick, too much on the surface, and that Russia as a whole did not give up old attitudes and beliefs, did not begin to share western European civilization. Anyway, is it possible for a man who is himself a brute to teach civilization to others?

St Petersburg, now called Leningrad, owes many of its finest buildings to the Tsars who reigned during the century after Peter the Great. The Hermitage Museum here, attached to the Winter Palace, was built by the Italian architect Bartolommeo Rastrelli between 1754 and 1762.

below: *Castletown House, County Kildare, is considered to be one of the finest country houses in Ireland. It was built during the 1720s for William Connolly, Speaker of the Irish Parliament, and was also Italian work: the architect was Alessandro Galilei and the decorators were the brothers Francini.*

2 THE CULTURE OF GENTLEMEN

Eighteenth-century style

At first it was an age of palaces. Other kings tried to equal or surpass Versailles. The greatest nobles were hardly less grandiose. It became the age of fine country houses, less overpowering than palaces, but still spacious and dignified. Architects and decorators still worked in the classical styles which had been revived at the time of the Renaissance. As the century went on, their desire to copy Greek and Roman patterns became stronger still. There was less ornamentation, more reliance on proportion, balance, space; it could perhaps be said that the style was a simpler, purer interpretation of classical taste. It may have been that educated people believed in Reason, calm, balanced humane thinking, as the best guide in life, and that classical civilization, in its architecture as well as in its literature, expressed this ideal most completely.

There is the same quality in town architecture, for example, in Britain. Though few towns retain so much of their eighteenth-century character as Bath, most towns which were important then can still boast some fine terraces; sometimes arranged in crescents or squares looking towards lawns and trees, but even in busy modern streets still showing a quiet superiority. All three capitals of England, Scotland and Ireland owe many of their finest streets and buildings to the architects of that time.

left: *Hanover Square, London, is a good example of early Georgian town development. It was promoted between 1717 and 1720 by Richard Lumley, Earl of Scarborough, and is shown in a print dated 1787.*

right: *Schönbrunn Palace, just outside Vienna, was built for the Emperor by one of Austria's greatest architects, J. B. Fischer von Erlach, in 1695 and the years after. This painting of the garden front was made by Bernardo Bellotto in 1759.*

It is possible to imagine the quality of life in such houses. Some have been turned into museums, furnished and decorated as they must have been when first they were lived in, and other museums have eighteenth-century 'period' rooms. The paint and paper on the walls, the design and workmanship of the furniture tell us of the taste of the people who bought and used them. So do the smaller objects – candlesticks, knives, forks and spoons, plates and china ornaments, clocks. Even remembering that one can presume the most highly valued objects are the ones to have been preserved and put on show, we may conclude that these things were made in an elegant age.

Compare the dress of these people with the fashions of the seventeenth and sixteenth centuries. It is still rich and elaborate, and the white wigs are more artificial than anything earlier. But now the lace and silk and jewellery is less obvious, the display is more subtle. These people believe that it is good manners to be controlled, restrained in dress as in all else.

Fashionable people made an art of conversation; good talk should be clear, accurate, witty. They danced the gavotte and minuet. They listened to the music of Handel, Bach, Mozart. They were civilized, cultured – and they knew it.

left: This painting by Michel Ollivier (1712–84) shows an elegant gathering at the Princess de Conti's Paris house in 1763. Tea in the English fashion is being served — the picture is entitled 'Le Thé à l'anglaise' — and one of the musicians entertaining the company is seven-year-old Mozart.

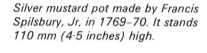

Silver mustard pot made by Francis Spilsbury, Jr, in 1769–70. It stands 110 mm (4·5 inches) high.

English furniture of the eighteenth century. A Chippendale-designed chair of about 1760, a chest of drawers of the same date and a wall cabinet of about 1740. All are of dark mahogany, a most fashionable wood at the time, and the fittings are of a gold-coloured alloy called ormolu.

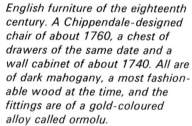

The battle of Fontenoy, 11 May 1745, painted by L. N. van Blavenberghe to hang in the palace of Versailles. It was a French victory, but the British infantry kept perfect formation under murderous fire, and their attack was only stopped by the charge of Irish regiments in the French service. This picture shows the well-drilled pattern of an eighteenth-century battle, but also the blinding smoke which could easily cause confusion – especially if troops on opposite sides, like the British and the Irish in this battle, were wearing uniforms of similar colour.

They even managed to give a civilized appearance to warfare. War was regarded as being a quarrel between governments which had to be settled by force, but there was no reason why this should make people behave like savages. The wars were fought by professional soldiers who knew what they were doing when they enlisted, and civilians were not involved, apart from the damage that unavoidably occurred in siege and battle. Armies were drilled until they could form lines and squares and perform complicated movements on the battlefield as exactly as on the parade ground. There is a well-known story of how, at the battle of Fontenoy in 1745, a British regiment came face to face with a French one; the two commanding officers bowed and each politely invited the other to fire first. Foreigners were not imprisoned just because their government happened to be at war with the government of the country where they were staying. When the writer Laurence Sterne fell ill, his doctors sent him to the south of France, though Britain and France had been at war for years, and he was warmly welcomed by French society. Admiral Rodney's French friends, by paying his debts, helped him to return to England when war broke out so that he could command British ships against French.

The seamy side

Of course there was another side to the eighteenth century. Those soldiers who fought such gentlemanly wars stood while cannon-balls, grapeshot and musketry volleys were tearing bloody holes in their closely ordered ranks. Why did they not run away? Courage and pride, but also fear of flogging and execution; and because they had been trained to obey orders almost automatically. Casualties were frightful, medical services cruelly inadequate. Pay was bad, pensions few. As for the

British navy, the writer Samuel Johnson wondered why any man should join it if he could manage to get himself hanged instead; and this was no joke. Yet, though the Royal Navy had to recruit men forcibly in time of war, armies and navies commonly managed to find volunteers.

Why did men join? Some were deceived or made drunk by the recruiting sergeants, no doubt, but for many it was a way of escape from poverty, misery and starvation. Most of the people of eighteenth-century Europe were countryfolk — peasant farmers, labourers, shepherds, foresters. For them, life was probably much as it always had been: hard work in the open air to grow their food, handing over a big share (anything from a tenth to a half) to the lord and the Church, constantly dreading bad harvests and the famines that so often came after. This was country life as it always had been for the ordinary people. It was no worse now than it had been, and in most parts of Europe things were probably rather better. Feudal lords were losing power in some districts, and governments were coming to realize that a kingdom would not be strong if the countryside was ailing. Some areas, though, suffered special hardship. Ireland was persecuted besides being poor; Irishmen in their thousands went to serve in the Catholic armies of France, Spain and Austria, while thousands more joined the British army.

Everyday life was hard. Perhaps half the babies born never reached adulthood, and relatively few reached old age. The registers and gravestones of parish churches often tell the story. The upper classes shared some of the dangers and pains of the lower. Smallpox, the great killer disease of that century, was no respecter of wealth. Indeed, to be rich enough to afford the services of a surgeon could easily mean not cure, but increased suffering; there were no anaesthetics, except strong drink. There was little sympathy for those who were victims of mental illness. Though they were no longer thought of as being possessed by devils, lunatics were often treated as though they could be made to behave themselves by punishment. In London there was a large hospital for the mad called Bethlehem or Bedlam; it was one of the sights, where many came to laugh at the crazy antics of the patients. A village idiot was probably treated with more kindness by his neighbours.

There were great cities in the eighteenth century, and in these life could be seen at its worst, as well as at its best. Crowding together more and more in filthy slums which grew as the cities grew, the poor may easily have felt more wretched – is there any way of measuring? – and sunk into drunkenness, vice and crime. There was little mercy for criminals who were caught. Most prisons were places where every sort of offender, from the helpless to the hardened, was simply locked away to rot. Torture was legal in most states, and the death penalty common; executions, ranging from hanging to breaking on the wheel, were in public – intended as warnings, they were usually regarded as entertainments.

There are contrasts in almost every society, almost every century, but it would be difficult to find sharper contradictions than those of the eighteenth century. Could any society go on like this, could the differences be reduced, or would there sooner or later be a breakdown?

Bedlam. The final scene in a series called 'The Rake's Progress' which William Hogarth painted and first engraved in 1735; it proved popular, and was reissued in later years. It tells how a foolish young man wastes his fortune and comes to poverty, prison and finally the madhouse. Here he is the central figure, chained because of his violence, abandoned by all except a faithful country girl who had been his first love. Hogarth also shows lunatics with political, religious, scientific and musical crazes, and fashionable ladies come for amusement.

25

The Enlightenment

British liberty

'Britons never, never, never shall be slaves!' The original was written in 1740, and there seems little doubt that most people in Britain who ever thought about it, and many people of other countries too, believed that Britain was a state where the people had more freedom than anywhere else in Europe — or possibly in the world. What were the reasons for this?

While most European states were ruled by despotic kings, a constitutional king reigned over Britain. Stuart kings had tried to rule despotically and had failed. The new family, which inherited the throne, with the permission of Parliament, came from Hanover. George I (1714-27) preferred to live in his German lands, and to a lesser extent George II (1727-60) felt the same. As long as things went fairly smoothly, they were quite willing to leave the running of their new kingdom to the party that had given them the crown, the Whigs.

There had been another party, the Tories. But the Tories had fallen into such confusion in 1714, when they could not decide whether they supported the Hanoverian or the Stuart family, that few people could trust in Toryism for the next half-century. The Tories had believed in supporting royal power and the Church of England. The Whigs believed that Parliament should be at least as powerful as the king, and that it was safest if nobody was too strong — a kind of balance of power within the state. The government, they thought, should prevent crime and disorder, but apart from that it should leave its subjects to lead their own lives. This was what the Whigs understood as liberty.

The Whig Party was not like the organized, disciplined and massive parties of the twentieth century. It was more like several groups of lords and members of Parliament (M.P.s), often relatives or friends, who agreed to follow one leader for as long as his conduct suited them. In return, he would promise them rewards and jobs if he became the king's minister. The man who was shrewd enough to keep most supporters together could be reasonably sure that King George would approve of him, and so he would be allowed to pick the other ministers in the king's government. He, of course, would be recognized as the first, or prime, minister.

Though the title of Prime Minister was to remain unofficial for two centuries, in fact the first British Prime Minister is usually thought to have been Sir Robert Walpole, who took charge in 1721 and ran the government for twenty-one years. Perhaps 'ran' is the wrong word. A true Whig, he never interfered if he could possibly avoid it. He worked on the old saying 'Let sleeping dogs lie'. He knew that sometimes an attempt to improve a situation only stirred up trouble and made the position worse, while a problem that was left alone sometimes turned out not to be very serious after all.

This suited the Whig lords and gentlemen. They believed in liberty, and this meant liberty for themselves in particular. Being rich and influential, they did not need the government to step in to protect them. And the less work the government did, the less money it needed in taxes. All the same, simply doing nothing would not have kept Walpole in power for two decades. He had to make sure that no one else took his place. He did it in various ways: by dismissing any other minister who showed signs of being able and ambitious; by keeping on friendly terms with the king and queen; and by using the crown's powers of patronage.

To persuade the king
to appoint him Prime Minister

A politician had to gather enough followers
to make it likely that he would win votes in both
Houses of Parliament.

Once appointed, he could use the king's powers of
patronage to buy extra support.

An anti-Walpole cartoon of 1733. He had proposed a scheme for raising money by an excise charge on certain goods, including tobacco. His opponents alleged that he would soon tax everything and cripple trade, and that he would use the money to hire excise-collectors and troops to oppress Britain. Here we see the lion and the unicorn, symbols of England, reduced to servitude. They are carrying a soldier and drawing an exciseman who rides in triumph on a barrel of tobacco. The depressed figure on the left represents Trade, and behind is a standing army. A breeze labelled 'Interest' (meaning influence and possibly corruption) blows over Westminster Hall (Parliament) towards St James's Palace (the king). Propaganda like this did succeed in frightening so many people that Walpole decided to drop his Excise Bill.

Walpole's bribery was not just a crude handing over of money, but more the giving of official jobs or pensions or titles to the friends and relatives of men whose support he wanted. In theory, these favours were given by the king; in practice, the First Lord of the Treasury – that was Walpole's official position – could depend on the king to follow his advice in such matters. It was corrupt, and many people said so, loudly. But it worked. As long as Walpole had the king and the majority of Parliament with him, his critics were helpless.

Besides buying the support of lords and M.P.s, it was possible to 'fix' elections to the House of Commons. Many M.P.s were elected by the counties, two for each shire. In the counties, all men who owned freehold land worth forty shillings a year had the right to vote. In the later Middle Ages, when this qualification had been laid down, such a freeholder would have been a reasonably prosperous man – the idea being that only men of a certain degree of wealth and responsibility ought to have a say in taxation and legislation. By Walpole's time forty shillings meant considerably less. In most counties

these freeholders were numbered in thousands. All the same, as many of these voters were fairly poor, it was often worth while for a candidate to try outright bribery, promises or threats. It would be a brave voter, for example, who dared to vote against the advice of the local squire – who was probably

'Calais Gate', or 'The Roast Beef of Old England', painted by Hogarth in 1749. A French cook, weak and staggering, carries the meat past scrawny soldiers (one of them an Irishman) and a woebegone Highland exile. The only one who seems to be prospering is the fat friar who lovingly fingers the beef. Hogarth shows himself sketching in the background, and the shadow beside him belongs to an official who did in fact arrest the artist on suspicion of making drawings of the fortifications.

often regarded as 'knowing best' anyway. Since all voting was done in public, there was no chance of pretending.

Other M.P.s were elected by those towns which had at various times in the past been named as parliamentary boroughs; as in the counties, two per borough. But here there was no general rule about who could vote; every borough had its own methods. Usually, though, the right to elect M.P.s belonged to a small group of wealthy townsmen – perhaps the mayor and corporation, or the freemen. Several boroughs were so weak that local landowners could always tell them which candidates to elect; it was well known that some lords had a number of boroughs 'in their pockets'.

In fact, because of all these conditions and arrangements in counties and boroughs, most M.P.s were probably returned unopposed at election time.

King and Parliament, Prime Minister and Whig lords and gentlemen worked well together. True, there were often bitter personal quarrels and rivalries, but these were within the system. They would all defend their aristocratic parliamentary monarchy against attack from outside. The Jacobites, the supporters of the exiled Stuart kings, twice tried to overthrow the Hanoverians by armed revolts, in 1715 and in 1745. The British upper classes would have nothing to do with them; only in the Scottish Highlands, where the whole way of life was different and the chieftains feared that the Whig system was going to weaken their hold over their clans, was there effective support for the rebels. As for the ordinary people, there is no sign that most of them wanted to rise, even in Scotland. (Ireland might have been different, but the native Irish were so completely kept under that they gave no trouble.)

Did the failures of these two revolutions mean that Walpole's policy had been wise? Were the British reasonably content? Did they see Britain, compared with other lands, as the home of liberty? Comparison was easiest with France, just across the Channel. British people thought they knew the differences. In France a man could be thrown into prison without trial, at the order of the king; nobles had privileges in the courts of justice, and they paid fewer taxes; in France there was no Parliament to hear complaints and vote down a bad government; there the Catholic Church was rich, and Protestants were victimized; in France, honest and prosperous merchants were not respected, but despised and insulted by the nobles, and people could not better themselves through brains and industry; ordinary French people were generally half-starved and servile — and British soldiers and sailors, especially sailors, could always thrash them. Ruling the waves was part of Britannia's freedom.

Hogarth sums up a great deal of this attitude; not the whole truth but, like a good caricature, near enough to be easily recognizable. As we have seen already, he knew the bad side of British life, too. But in his frank view of an election he shows us men who, with all their violence and corruption, are vigorous and free. Not all elections were bought and sold. Westminster especially was famed as a place where the ordinary people elected the men they wanted, and when popular

In 1755 Hogarth painted a series of four stages in an election: first, the candidates giving a feast to the electors, next canvassing for votes, then the polling itself at the hustings, and lastly the rowdy procession as the winners are carried in triumph by their supporters. This is the second, and shows the candidate addressing himself to the ladies and ignoring the corrupt deals that are being made nearby.

feeling ran high in London the government usually took it seriously. It was quite possible to rise, too. Many of the leading men of the century had begun life in non-aristocratic families, and had won fame and fortune in their professions, or business, or even politics by hard work, brains, courage and luck. Rightly or wrongly, there were many very ordinary people in eighteenth-century Britain who believed that they were free.

There was plenty of selfishness and brutality in this free country, but there were people who tried to make improvements. Some experimented with improved methods of farming, some tried to find better ways of manufacturing such things as iron and cloth. These experiments were to develop into great changes which have been called the Agricultural and Industrial Revolutions, which in turn changed the way of life of most of mankind. That is a subject which is too big to be discussed here, and anyway its full effects were not obvious until the next century. The men who made these improvements were not unselfish; most of them wanted to be rich, or richer. Other improvers were concerned to help those to whom freedom had brought few blessings.

Thomas Coram, a retired sea-captain, after many years of effort, established in 1739 the Foundling Hospital in London 'to prevent the frequent murders of poor miserable children at their birth, and to suppress the inhuman custom of exposing new-born infants to perish in the streets,' as his petition for a royal charter explains. About the same time General James Oglethorpe was busy establishing in Georgia a colony where debtors could be helped to start a new life. In the 1770s John Howard succeeded in beginning a movement to improve conditions in prisons, and in the 1780s William Wilberforce became leader of a movement to abolish slavery and the slave trade. While these practical philanthropists were trying to reduce physical suffering, there was a movement led by the brothers John and Charles Wesley to bring the teachings of the Church of England into the lives of the mass of ordinary people, preaching like the early friars in streets and markets. Eventually they were forced out of the Church of England, and their Methodism became another new branch of the Christian religion; it was caused, as the Wesleys saw it, by a very practical need.

Reason in France

After the reign of Louis XIV there were many Frenchmen who thought that their own country could learn a great deal from Britain. Though they admired the practical attitude of British politicians, farmers, traders and philanthropists, Frenchmen who were interested in these matters usually preferred to work out the ideas fully in books, and thus influence the government, perhaps, to put the theories into practice.

It was easy enough to read what the British Whigs believed. Soon after the 'Glorious Revolution' of 1688 John Locke had published books to explain the theory behind what the Whigs had just done. He argued that kings had no special divine powers, but had to obey the laws like anybody else. He said that governments should be so balanced that no one man or group of men could behave despotically. French writers developed ideas that were very similar.

In *The Spirit of the Laws*, published in 1748, Baron Montesquieu expounded ideas which are usually simplified like this. In any state there are three vital powers:

the power to make laws, or *legislative* power;
the power to enforce the laws, or *executive* power;
the power to judge whether or not the law has been
  broken, or *judicial* power.

These powers, he said, must always be kept separate. If more than one fell into the hands of an individual or group, that could lead to despotism and tyranny.

Montesquieu was one of a number of highly intelligent and educated Europeans who held what were called 'Enlightened' ideas. They believed that a government's task was to improve and enrich its country by assisting commerce, constructing roads and canals, encouraging better agriculture, fostering industries. Old customs which impeded progress should be swept away – for instance, it was a nuisance to have different laws and trade regulations in different parts of the same state. A government should remove obstacles to the prosperity of its subjects, but, as long as they were peaceful and orderly, should not interfere in their lives. People should be entitled to believe in whatever religion best suited their consciences, and the state should be fair to all. Some of this may sound rather like the ideas of the ancient Romans on tolerance and justice; remember that the classics were still the basis of education all over western Europe. Montesquieu himself wrote a book on the reasons for the rise and decline of the Romans.

Enlightened people shared the same general attitude, though they often disagreed on important matters. Some were devout Christians, others distrusted religion. Some wanted powerful governments that could enforce Enlightened policies;

above: *The illustration at the beginning of Buffon's second volume on birds.*

right: *From the Encyclopaedia, a diagram of labour-saving machinery at a slate mine. The horse-powered windlass is being used here to bail water out of the quarry, but it could also be used to hoist slates up to ground level.*

others wanted governments' powers to be severely limited. In different countries the problems and possibilities looked very different; Portugal, for instance, was quite unlike a little German principality. But we have room for only a few examples so, as France so often set the fashion, it seems best to consider the most famous of the French Enlightened writers.

One group are known as the Encyclopaedists because they contributed to a large new Encyclopaedia which was to contain the most up-to-date knowledge on everything that was useful – in their opinion, of course. By the time it was finished it was thirty-five volumes long, and eleven of these contain 3,000 large engravings which reveal in clear detail both technical processes and scientific knowledge.

Many French gentlemen were interested in studying nature, examining and classifying exactly. Count·Buffon produced thirty-six volumes of his Natural History between 1749 and his death in 1788, and another eight written by a colleague were still needed to complete it. Some of the work of French inventors in applying steam power to land and water transport, and in lighter-than-air flight is illustrated here. Science was not only practical, it was becoming fashionable. Well-educated gentlemen – and ladies too, who held 'salons' where the guests were supposed to be interested and informed and able to talk about literature and the arts – now kept up with the ideas of

In 1769 N. J. Cugnot, a French military engineer, made a steam locomotive which could move along a road at 3·25 km per hour (2·25 m.p.h.). The government ordered him to make a new version, of which this is a model, to pull artillery. Though it was built at the Paris Arsenal it was never brought into service.

below: *A contemporary picture of the first flight by human beings, at Paris on 21 November 1783. This balloon was one of the hot-air type, invented by the Montgolfier brothers. Ten days later a hydrogen-filled balloon, invented by Professor Charles, made an even more successful flight, also from Paris.*

This picture, from a French journal of 1816, shows a more successful attempt to use steam power for transport. The Marquis Jouffroy d'Abbans made a steamboat which in the 1780s plied successfully on the Saône, near Lyons, for about fifteen months.

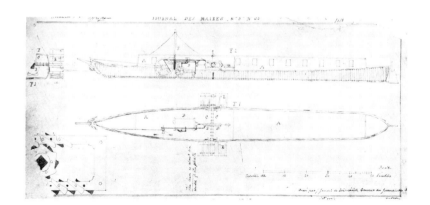

above: *François-Marie Arouet de Voltaire, 1694–1778. Bust by J. A. Houdon, the foremost French sculptor of the time.*

right: *A contemporary engraving entitled 'The Unhappy Calas Family', and obviously intended to arouse sympathy for them.*

scientists. The ideas of Sir Isaac Newton, who had died in 1727 at the ripe age of eighty-five, were accepted respectfully as the foundation of a scientific understanding of the world.

The Encyclopaedists, on the whole, were not content to accept science as a useful explanation of how nature worked. They tended to see science as a substitute for religion, something which explained the universe without bringing in God; at least, if there were a god it would be some impersonal spirit of benevolence, quite unlike the usual Christian picture. It is not surprising that the Church condemned many of the books of Enlightened French authors. Equally, these authors lost no opportunity of attacking the Church. Articles in the Encyclopaedia were sometimes written in such a way as to lead the reader to share the author's beliefs about religion and politics. So the Encyclopaedia was not simply a great store of useful information; it was also propaganda.

Why did Enlightened Frenchmen so dislike the Church? Mainly, it seems, because the Church tried to prevent people from making up their own minds about what was right and true in religion. The Church was behind things like Louis XIV's Revocation of the Edict of Nantes, cruel as well as stupid. The Church distrusted anyone who asked questions and muzzled scientists. The Church was enormously rich, and wasted money supporting a crowd of lazy priests and monks and nuns instead of helping trade and industry. There was plenty of evidence to support these charges. There was also a great deal of evidence for the defence, but that was never presented with anything like the skill of the Enlightened writers.

The man who did most to show up all the weaknesses of the Church was Voltaire, a very prolific writer with a gift for making sarcastic remarks. Voltaire loathed stupidity, prejudice and injustice. He found plenty of targets for his jibes, and constantly was in trouble; he was exiled, sent to cool down in the Bastille, and fled to avoid arrest on a number of occasions. One of his most famous fights was the Calas case.

Calas was a shopkeeper in Toulouse. He was accused of murdering one of his sons and, though he denied it even under torture, was found guilty and broken on the wheel. Calas was a Protestant, and the prosecutor alleged that the son had been about to turn Catholic when the father killed him. When Voltaire was told of the case he realized that much of the evidence had been twisted. He began to write furious attacks on the Toulouse judges who had been ready to believe anything bad about Calas because he did not belong to their Church. After a struggle that went on for years, Voltaire won. The case was re-investigated. Calas was declared innocent. The unfortunate man could not be restored to life, but his family had their name cleared and his property returned to them.

Though it had not been priests and bishops, but lawyers and judges, who had been responsible for Calas' agonized death, it was the Church that was blamed. This was the sort of thing that happened when people became religious bigots and did not use their reason. Though Voltaire did not actually say so, there was a strong suggestion that you could not be religious and reasonable; religion and reason would not mix.

Nature and sentiment

Can a civilization be *too* civilized? Can people become so very restrained and reasonable and polite that the whole thing seems too artificial, affected and unnatural to be endured?

Some members of the upper classes could find relief in the brutality and excitement of hunting, drinking and gambling. Some poets and artists tried to put more plain natural feeling, even violent emotion at times, into their work. They showed a new interest in the countryside and the changing seasons, they began to revive old legends and ballads about heroes and knights. Some pictures were intended deliberately to appeal to people's softer sentiments. At Versailles itself Queen Marie Antoinette in the 1780s played at 'the simple life' on a little farm built specially for her in the park. Some of this was as artificial and insincere as anything that had been done before, but there is no doubt that many people, in different ways, felt that eighteenth-century civilization was missing something.

One writer especially felt that civilization had done more harm than good, and that if people would only live naturally and freely they would be honest, happy and generous. His name was Jean-Jacques Rousseau, a French-speaking Swiss who was highly emotional, muddle-headed and self-centred; he wrote well, and fascinated his readers.

'Girl with a Dead Bird', painted by J. B. Greuze, whose sentimental work was very popular in the later eighteenth century.

The myth of 'the noble savage' was not new. Almost from the moment Columbus returned from his first voyage there had been Europeans who compared the virtues of the simple Indian with the vices of the corrupt European. Some French writers in the eighteenth century told idealized stories of life by the Mississippi, and the newly discovered islands of the South Seas sounded like paradise. So readers may have been already half disposed to accept what Rousseau preached.

In one famous book, *Emile*, Rousseau tried to show how an individual would grow up into a fine adult if allowed to develop freely instead of being forced at school to do what others wanted. Even more famous was the book in which he explained his ideas about people in the mass, in states. The

book was called *The Social Contract*, and began: 'Man is born free, but everywhere he is in chains.' It is the sort of sentence that gets remembered and quoted, even if the meaning is not perfectly clear. Rousseau said that the people – by which he seems to have meant everybody living in a particular country – must always remain free, their own masters, their own sovereign. There was an understanding, a kind of unwritten contract between the people and their ruler that they would obey as long as he carried out their wishes. But if the government went against *the general will*, it lost its rights and could be thrown out.

Rousseau's ideas, even more than Locke's, were a contradiction of the Divine Right of Kings. He was vague about important practical details, such as what exactly the general will was and how a government could try to discover it. But he was easy to read and talk about. In the salons he was a fashionable author. Privileged nobles saw no harm in discussing the ideas. Were they really so shocking? After all, since so much was vague, the king himself could argue that he, representing the people as a whole, was best fitted to declare the general will!

The Social Contract was published in 1762. In view of what was to happen in thirty years, it may seem that the French upper classes were blind to what it really meant. But that would hardly be fair. The civilized people who were accustomed to the reasonings of the Enlightenment would naturally take Rousseau's as another interesting set of ideas to discuss. Besides, it is very difficult to decide how far Rousseau's book persuaded anybody to do anything. Did his ideas bring about great events or were they merely a sign of the times?

Omai was the first South Sea Islander to visit Britain, and in 1776 this portrait of him was exhibited in the Royal Academy. It is by no less a person than Sir Joshua Reynolds, the first President of the Royal Academy.

The Enlightened Despots

Kings can be just as intelligent and well-educated as anybody else. Often they have been very intelligent indeed. Several monarchs in different countries were as interested as any of their subjects in the ideas of the Enlightenment, and in various ways they acted upon them.

Frederick II of Prussia

Frederick William I's son hated everything to do with his sergeant-major of a father (pages 16-17). He liked music, read the latest books, and spoke French rather than German. Once he tried to run away, but was caught. He and a friend who helped him were classed as army officers, and therefore guilty of desertion. Frederick saw his friend being beheaded and was made to expect the same fate himself: he was finally spared, only because he was needed as the Crown Prince.

Frederick had no choice but to wait for his father to die. Meanwhile he read and wrote. In 1740 he published, anonymously, a book condemning the unscrupulous political ideas of the Italian writer and statesman Machiavelli. That same year the old king died, and Frederick now had the chance to show what an Enlightened ruler could do.

His first act was to disband his father's famous regiment of giants. But anybody who judged from this that the new king was full of peace and goodwill was badly mistaken. Frederick merely had no use for expensive ornaments. His was going to be a practical army.

Brandenburg-Prussia was mostly poor land. Just to the south lay Silesia, fertile and rich in minerals. Frederick marched his army into Silesia and claimed it.

Silesia was Habsburg territory, and had been since 1526. But Emperor Charles VI (page 15) had no son, only a daughter named Maria Theresa. There was some doubt as to whether a woman could inherit some of the Habsburg lands, so Charles had taken care to get all the leading states in Europe, including Prussia, to promise to allow Maria Theresa to inherit. Charles died a few months after Frederick's father and Frederick lost no time in breaking his promise.

This armed grab set off a series of wars lasting, off and on, for nearly a quarter of a century. The first, called the War of the

Silesia, Austria and Prussia, 1740

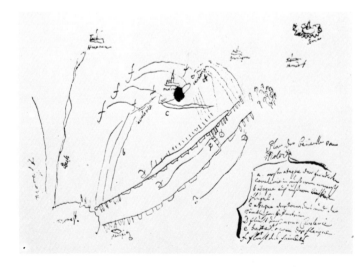

Plan of the battle of Mollwitz, 10 April 1741, sketched by Frederick in a letter he wrote shortly afterwards. It was his first battle. After an Austrian cavalry charge he thought all was lost, and fled. His army held on, and won. It was an unheroic beginning but he learned.

WAR OF AUSTRIAN SUCCESSION | DIPLOMATIC REVOLUTION | SEVEN YEARS' WAR

Austrian Succession, lasted from 1740 to 1748. In this war France, naturally, came in against Austria; and Britain, partly because of rivalry in the colonies, naturally sided against France. At the end of a lot of fighting in many parts of Europe and the world, peace was signed leaving Frederick in possession of Silesia.

Maria Theresa was determined to get it back. Her previous allies had not been of much use. Could she find better? Her chief adviser, Chancellor Prince Kaunitz, thought she could. Why not France? France had been the enemy for more than two centuries, but was there any longer a reason for the feud? It was time to face reality, that since Spain was no longer Habsburg the old fears and hopes were ended. When Kaunitz approached the French government, they agreed. So France and Austria became allies.

It may seem only commonsense, but to statesmen who had for so long been able to weave all their schemes round the one thing that was absolutely certain in international politics, the Habsburg–Bourbon feud, it was a staggering upset. It has rightly been called the Diplomatic Revolution.

Next Maria Theresa came to an understanding with Russia to join in war against Prussia, more actively this time.

Britain and Prussia agreed to help each other. They had to. Nobody else wanted them.

The Seven Years' War began in 1756. Once again Britain and France fought in their colonies, and we shall discuss this later. In Europe, despite some help from Britain and one or two small German states, Frederick faced an impossible task. Prussia had to meet the armies of three great powers, each far stronger than herself. The miracle of how Prussia survived may have something to do with the loyalty of the troops, whose discipline held them firm instead of causing desertions. It may partly be explained by Frederick himself, who turned out to be an extremely good general, while some of his opponents were just the reverse. But the strain was terrible. Enemy armies marched over Prussia, for a time the Russians were in Berlin. We have the story of Frederick screaming at his men as they recoiled from murderous musket fire: 'Dogs! Do you want to live for ever?' The situation became more desperate still when the new Tory government which ruled Britain after 1760 began preparing to make peace with France. Courage and skill were not enough to save Frederick, but luck rescued him. In 1762 a young prince became Tsar who hero-worshipped the warrior king of Prussia. At once he pulled back the Russian armies.

Maria Theresa recognized that there was now no hope of breaking Frederick. Peace was signed in 1763, and Silesia belonged to Prussia.

Frederick II of Prussia has been blamed for doing great harm to Europe. It has been said that he broke his word, behaved like a robber – and won. This was very bad for international honesty and trust, it is said. But was Frederick really so much worse than others? Or was he perhaps rather less hypocritical? He has also been blamed for finally turning Prussia into a militaristic state. Certainly his victories became a source of pride to his people, and eventually the Prussians had the reputation of practically worshipping the army. But did other nations never boast of military glory? And was it all the doing of Frederick alone?

Whatever the fairest judgment may be, 'Old Fritz' became a hero to the Prussians. His wars had meant the gaining of

The wars are over. The ageing Frederick, in his Prussian blue uniform and attended by cavalry officers, has turned his attention to making his kingdom prosper, and is here inspecting plans for mining galleries. Contemporary painting by J. C. Frisch.

reasonably valuable territory at enormous cost, but they had also shown beyond a shadow of doubt that from now on Prussia must be treated as one of the great military powers. Perhaps this was something that they really valued.

Even during his campaigns Frederick had remained Enlightened. He read the latest French books, exchanged letters with authors like Voltaire, and had some of them stay at his court. Now at peace, he had a chance to show if these Enlightened ideas had any practical meaning to him.

He tried to make Prussia prosperous. He gave help from army stores to badly wasted areas. He excused from taxes districts which had suffered bad harvests. He built new villages in places where the land had not been fully used previously. He encouraged foreign settlers, especially skilled workmen. He protected peasants against being thrown off the lands they tilled. He improved roads, made canals. He helped to begin or extend many industries – sugar, salt, starch, tobacco, wool, cotton, silk, paper, iron – and helped in setting up banks to provide financial lubrication for it all.

He insisted on justice for everyone, no matter how weak. On one famous occasion Frederick dismissed his chancellor and imprisoned some judges because he thought they had allowed a poor miller to be unjustly treated. He insisted that government officials should be well educated, and punished severely any he discovered to be incompetent or dishonest. All his sub-

jects could worship freely according to their own religious beliefs.

Prosperity, justice and honesty, freedom of religion – it all sounds as Enlightened as could be. But there was no question about who gave the orders.

The king wanted a well-run state because it would be strong. He would rule efficiently and fairly. In return he expected loyalty and obedience. Ordinary Prussians must work hard at their own business. Many of the peasants were still serfs, unable to leave their lord or their village; Frederick showed no sign of wanting to set them free. At the other end of the social scale he did nothing to curb the privileges and pride of the nobles and gentry; he relied on these people as his chief assistants, though he did make sure that they earned their position by hard, devoted work.

As far as Frederick II was concerned, Enlightened government was simply efficient government. It was for the good of people and government alike, because it meant that all would be prosperous and strong. But this had nothing to do with freedom, or parliaments. The king would decide what was good for everybody. Being Enlightened, he would decide aright, and therefore it was proper for him to be a despot. At least, that seemed a very reasonable argument to an Enlightened Despot.

Catherine II of Russia

Catherine was not a Russian, but a princess from a small north German state. In 1745, at the age of sixteen, she was married to a young prince connected to the Russian royal family. (This was the man whose succession to the Tsardom in 1762 saved Frederick II of Prussia.) Catherine had a long and lurid life which included the murder of her husband (who was not sane) and affairs with an almost incredible procession of lovers. This, however, did not prevent her being a very able and intelligent ruler who was determined to Enlighten her vast empire.

She had to work on and through the nobles, and she tried to make her courtiers follow French fashions – dress French, eat French, talk French, read French; perhaps eventually think French? She tried to persuade the nobles that they would benefit if they treated their serfs decently. Like Peter (and Frederick of Prussia) she tried to attract skilled foreigners. She wrote a complete set of instructions to show her ministers how they should rule, all based on the ideas of French Enlightened writers. She did not quite dare to abolish torture, but she ordered that no court should use it without imperial permission, and she did not grant permission.

Catherine meant well, and in her court there was the appearance, the polish of eighteenth-century style. But how far did it go? There is a story about how her favourite Potemkin was able to take the Tsarina on tours of his 'improved' villages; she did not realize that the neat buildings were sham, like film sets, and the happy peasants had been specially brought, like film extras. Was she really deceived? Or did she allow herself to be deceived because she depended so much upon her favourites? The court of St Petersburg was a world apart from the huts of peasants on the distant Volga, where things were much as always. During Catherine's reign there took place one of the great peasant uprisings which flare from time to time across Russian history. The leader, a Cossack named Pugachev, claimed to be the true Tsar, Catherine's murdered husband. It seems as though the thousands who joined him, so far from appreciating her Enlightened ideas, blamed Catherine for their miseries and the oppression of the nobles. For most of 1774 Pugachev spread terror and destruction from the Urals to central Russia before he was defeated and executed.

Catherine's 'greatness', as so often, refers not to any good

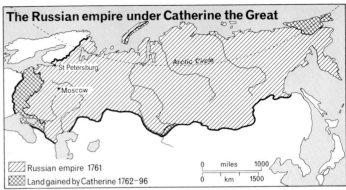

The Russian empire under Catherine the Great

- ▨ Russian empire 1761
- ▧ Land gained by Catherine 1762–96

0 ____ miles ____ 1000
0 ____ km ____ 1500

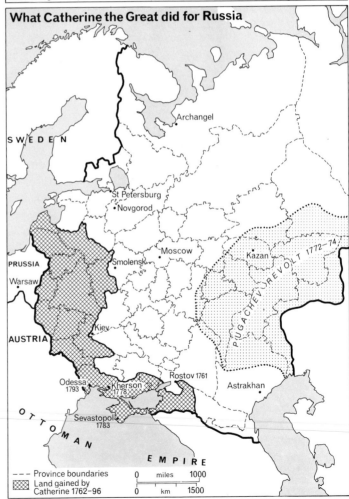

What Catherine the Great did for Russia

- --- Province boundaries
- ▧ Land gained by Catherine 1762–96

0 ____ miles ____ 1000
0 ____ km ____ 1500

Pugachev has been captured and is being taken to be tried, as shown in a contemporary print. His captors have caged him like a wild beast, but they have given him his pipe. Another contrast is between the traditional Russian appearance of the driver and the up-to-date escort.

right: *A contemporary French cartoon of 'The Cake of Kings'. King Stanislas Poniatowski protests vainly to Catherine II as she, Joseph II and Frederick II help themselves to slices of Poland.*

she may have tried to do her subjects, but to the territory she added to her empire. The map opposite shows her achievements, and there is no need to describe her wars against the Turks and Swedes. One of her 'grabs' however is unusually interesting.

Poland was large but weak. There was no hereditary crown: every time a king died the nobles had the right to choose the new one. In the assembly of nobles every member had the right of veto; any one man could forbid business to go on. It is easy to understand how, while kings all around were strengthening their powers, the Polish crown was weak. Catherine had the opportunity to dominate Poland completely, but she understood the Balance of Power, that her neighbours could never allow Russia alone to grow. She therefore invited

Prussia and Austria to share. As the map on the next page shows, in three stages over twenty-three years Poland was totally cut up and swallowed.

The Partitions of Poland have often been condemned as a great crime against the Polish nation. But this meant nothing to Catherine and her accomplices. To educated people of the eighteenth century the important things about a man were his culture, social position and wealth, not his nationality. Catherine was merely trying to profit from a state which was obviously incapable of looking after itself. But the shock of being partitioned and ruled by foreigners, especially their old enemies the Russians, aroused in many Poles a passionate desire for the national independence they had lost. The nobles had long been proudly independent, but in a selfish way which had destroyed the independence of their nation. This gradually became less powerful than a new feeling that the nation must come first, that any sacrifice was worth making in the cause of national freedom. Despite all their efforts, the Poles were to remain a subject nation for more than a century. But the spirit of nationalism, which other peoples were soon to share, was to be as great a force in the politics of Europe as the careful balances and calculations of the Enlightened kings and statesmen.

39

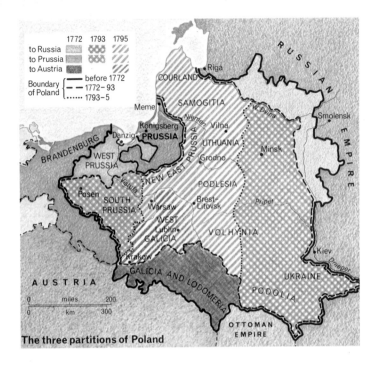

The three partitions of Poland

Map legend:
to Russia — 1772 1793 1795
to Prussia
to Austria
Boundary of Poland — before 1772 / 1772–93 / 1793–5

Joseph II of Austria

The son of Maria Theresa, though willing enough to increase his territories if he got the chance, was not a conquering warrior. Everyone who met him found him pleasant, kind, intelligent. His mother had begun seriously to try to make the nobles in her different lands pay a fair share of the taxes, and to persuade the Church to devote more of its wealth to practical tasks in the parishes instead of decorating great monasteries and churches. This may have seemed Enlightened, but it was not anti-noble or anti-Church. New colleges were founded for the education of the nobility, and Church money was kept for Church purposes. What Maria Theresa and Joseph wanted were 'God-pleasing justice' and 'God-pleasing equality'. After his mother's death in 1780 Joseph II was sole ruler, and felt free to bring in all the improvements he had been preparing.

In 1790 Joseph himself died, unpopular and a failure. What had gone wrong? It is easy enough to see why nobles and some of the clergy opposed him, because they feared that they would lose wealth and power, particularly when he abolished serf-

dom in Austria. But why did Joseph become unpopular with ordinary people who stood to gain from his reforms?

One reason was that his Enlightened behaviour was too despotic. He wanted only one new system of government to cover all his varied lands, and does not seem to have understood that people liked their own old customs precisely because they were their own and had been for a long time; they felt that the Emperor's bright new plans were going to make them just like any other of his subjects, instead of Netherlanders or Tyroleans or Bohemians. Many of the peasants disliked attempts to 'improve' the Church they had been brought up to respect as something sure and permanent, and disapproved of Joseph's toleration of *all* Christian religions. On the other hand, many of the Enlightened writers in Vienna criticized Joseph's toleration because it excluded non-Christians. They also became disillusioned because, though Joseph relaxed the censorship, he made it quite clear that he had no intention of taking any notice of pamphleteers, journalists and playwrights; he knew best. Many people were uneasy about his reforms in the treatment of criminals, too; he commuted death sentences, but he increased what he thought would be more effective lessons, like hard labour or public humiliation. There seemed to be something in Joseph which prevented him from appreciating fully the ideas and feelings of other people. He wanted to do good, but in a *doctrinaire* way, that is according to a fixed set of ideas which he had worked out long before and from which he would not swerve.

Joseph's crowning mistake was being drawn by Catherine of Russia into a war against the Turks. Austria got little out of it, and Joseph had to impose very heavy taxes to pay for his unpopular war.

Joseph II was a good man but a poor politician.

Though few tried to go as far as Joseph II, many kings, from Spain to Denmark, tried to run their states according to Enlightened ideas. They saw that to simplify laws, encourage industries, and restrict the privileges which some classes had collected over the centuries would strengthen their own governments. Yet there is no need to assume that they did not really care about the welfare of their subjects. In the century since Louis XIV kings had not become less despotic, but they had picked up some new ideas about the duties of an efficient government.

Two sides of
Joseph II's
Enlightenment.
Right, *an early
nineteenth-
century engraving
of the Vienna
General Hospital,
built in 1784.*
Below, *a
contemporary
engraving of how
Joseph tried to
cure prostitutes:
arrested, tried,
heads shaved and
sent with brooms
to sweep the
streets.*

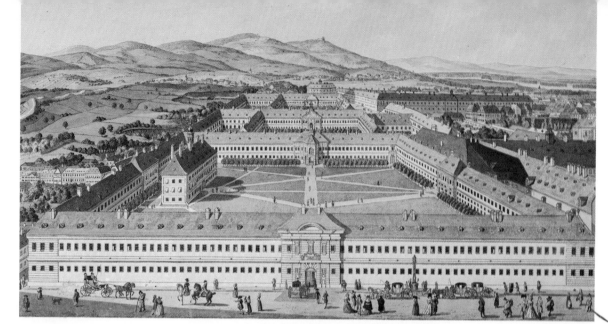

3 EUROPE OVERSEAS

The rise of the British Empire

It may seem that eighteenth-century Europe was a little closed circle, entirely concerned with its own politics and culture. But there was a world outside, and many Europeans were well aware of it, even if most of their attention was taken up with matters nearer home. Interest in other parts of the world varied from country to country. Since the great discoveries of the fifteenth and sixteenth centuries trade and settlement had grown. By the early eighteenth century the Portuguese, Spaniards and Dutch all had as much as they could manage, and had also shown that they could hold on to what they had. Smaller maritime powers like the Danes and Prussians were content mainly to trade, and wanted only a few posts. There remained Britain and France, both still unsatisfied and both active in the same parts of the world.

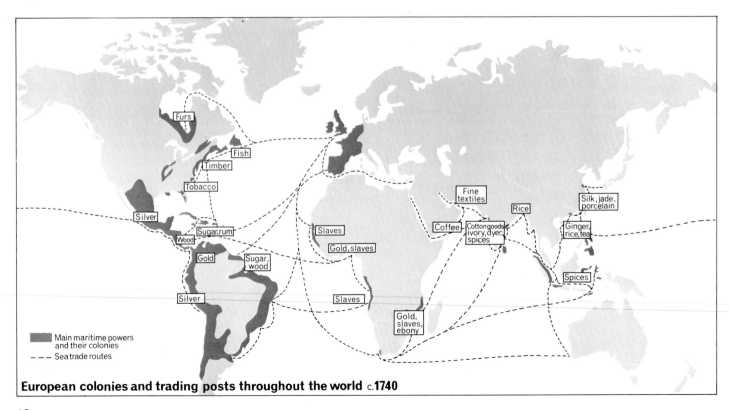

European colonies and trading posts throughout the world c.1740

Furs
Fish
Timber
Tobacco
Silver
Sugar, rum
Wood
Gold
Sugar, wood
Silver
Slaves
Gold, slaves
Slaves
Gold, slaves, ebony
Coffee
Fine textiles
Cotton goods, ivory, dyes, spices
Rice
Silk, jade, porcelain
Ginger, rice, tea
Spices

Main maritime powers and their colonies
- - - Sea trade routes

The struggle for India

The East had always been the great source of wealth for Western merchants. China and Japan had closed their doors to the white barbarians and the Dutch were firmly established in the East Indies. India remained. Here the Mogul emperors had permitted 'factories' or trading posts to be set up by various European companies.

While the Moguls were strong, the traders were quite secure. But their empire began to weaken. The Mahrattas, a race of Hindu horsemen, formed a group of warlike states across the middle of the subcontinent. By the old north-west route came new invaders, and Delhi itself fell, for a time, to the Afghans. With the central power so weak, the local rulers or 'nawabs' were left to do very much as they pleased. In these circumstances the trading companies strengthened the defences of their factories. They recruited Indians and trained them to fight in the European way; these troops were called 'sepoys', and soon showed that they were far more useful than the nawabs' troops. Next the governors of factories began to interfere in local Indian politics so as to earn extra privileges for themselves and to harm other companies.

The main factory of the French East India Company was Pondicherry, on the coast of the Carnatic, and the main British factory was not far away, at Madras. When the War of the Austrian Succession broke out in Europe the British and French in India were able to fight openly. Dupleix, the very able French commander, took Madras, but, much to his disgust, he had to give it back at the peace of 1748 in exchange for the fortress of Louisbourg in North America, which the British had taken.

Dupleix was disappointed, but he soon found a chance to move again, even though Britain and France were at peace. Rival princes claimed the throne of the Carnatic and war broke out between them. Dupleix supported one of them on the understanding that when he won he would use his authority as Nawab of the Carnatic to expel the British. With Dupleix's sepoys to help him, he was bound to win.

But real war is not like a game with rules and calculations, and this was one of the important moments in history when the certain winners lost. A discontented young clerk in Madras called Robert Clive turned soldier, collected a scratch force of British and Indians, and struck suddenly at the stronghold of Dupleix's prince. It was a desperate gamble, but it succeeded.

The great Mahratta leader Shivaji, with some of his warriors, is shown in a painting of the late seventeenth century. They are armed with spears, swords, daggers and circular shields. Some of the swords, including Shivaji's own, have the 'gauntlet' hilt used only by the Mahrattas, but otherwise this equipment, together with some bows and matchlock muskets, can be taken as normal for a native Indian army all through the eighteenth century. Often the weapons were of excellent quality and the warriors skilful and brave, but they were far less useful as soldiers than the sepoys, who carried only a flintlock musket and bayonet each but who had European discipline and drill. The sepoy shown on the left belongs to the East India Company's Bombay force, and the print is dated 1773.

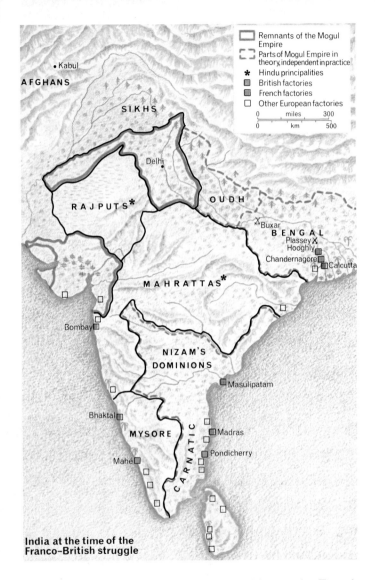

India at the time of the
Franco–British struggle

Map legend:
- Remnants of the Mogul Empire
- Parts of Mogul Empire in theory, independent in practice
- * Hindu principalities
- British factories
- French factories
- Other European factories

miles 300 / km 500

Labels on map: Kabul, AFGHANS, SIKHS, Delhi, RAJPUTS*, OUDH, Buxar, BENGAL, Plassey X, Hooghly, Chandernagore, Calcutta, MAHRATTAS*, Bombay, NIZAM'S DOMINIONS, Masulipatam, Bhaktal, MYSORE, CARNATIC, Madras, Pondicherry, Mahé

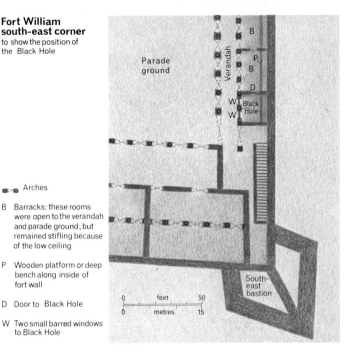

**Fort William
south-east corner**
to show the position of the Black Hole

Labels: Parade ground, Verandah, Black Hole, B, P, B, D, W, W, South-east bastion

Arches

B Barracks: these rooms were open to the verandah and parade ground, but remained stifling because of the low ceiling

P Wooden platform or deep bench along inside of fort wall

D Door to Black Hole

W Two small barred windows to Black Hole

feet 50 / metres 15

The other prince won the Carnatic, and it was the French Company which now found itself at a disadvantage.

This was the turning point. Though during later wars between Britain and France there were times when French troops and fleets made determined and skilful attempts to overthrow the British, they never managed it. The British East India Company held its advantage and steadily strengthened its position. Now it had learned the lesson that it had to be ready to fight to survive, and also that it was strong enough to win. The British government had also realized that it could not let the Company be defeated, and therefore sent king's ships and regiments to fight beside those of the Company. These powerful forces would obviously be used against any enemy, not merely against the French, and the Company soon found itself drawn deeper and deeper into Indian politics and wars. The struggle against France turned into a series of wars against Indian rulers and the conquest of wide lands with millions of people.

The first big conquest was not near Madras, but near another factory, Calcutta. In 1756 the Nawab of Bengal marched on Calcutta because the British, pleading fear of the French, refused to stop strengthening their fort. When the place fell 146 British were pushed for the night into the Black Hole of the fort, a cell which the British authorites used as a lock-up for drunk and disorderly soldiers. Of these, 123 suffocated. This famous 'atrocity story' has been used in the past to show how cruel and wicked Indian rulers could be, and so to justify British conquests. The truth seems to be that the nawab, admittedly an unpleasant young man detested by many of his

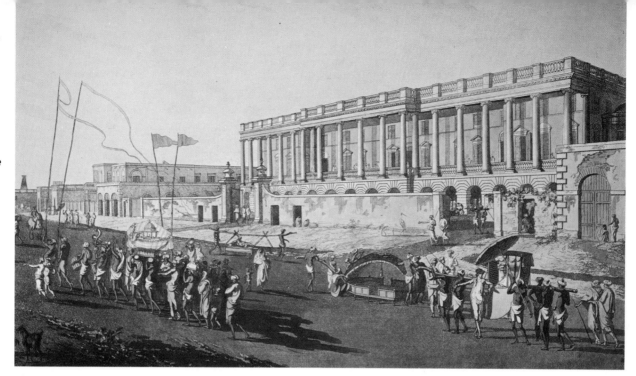

own people, had simply ordered the prisoners to be locked in the usual place without giving a thought to the conditions; the suffering and deaths were not planned. The result was that Clive brought an army and reoccupied Calcutta. At the battle of Plassey, 23 June 1757, Clive's army of 800 British soldiers and 2,200 sepoys defeated the nawab's 50,000. This at first looks like a splendid victory, a fit beginning to the empire which the British were about to build in India.

Certainly the British were about to build their Indian empire, but the truth was not so simple and heroic. The previous January Clive had made peace with the nawab, and had then made secret agreements with discontented Indian merchants and officials. So, when battle was joined, one wing of the nawab's army refused to fight, and many of the rest showed little enthusiasm. Afterwards the general who had held back received his reward. He became the new nawab.

The British too had their rewards. Clive got a gift of £234,000. The Company got a large stretch of land which yielded a large rent. British merchants were allowed to trade anywhere in Bengal without paying taxes – which gave them an enormous advantage over all Indian and other merchants,

below: *Sir David Ochterlony, British Resident in Delhi, entertaining in Indian fashion. This painting, dating from about 1820, suggests that important British officials were still prepared to mix with Indians as equals – though perhaps the portraits on the wall suggest a hint of the disapproval that such conduct would arouse later in the nineteenth century.*

who had to pay the taxes. Greedy British wanted more than they had any reasonable claim to take, and some Indian officials and merchants worked with them. Others complained and at last the nawab tried to deprive the British of their privileged position.

It is easy for us now to see that no government could possibly allow a foreign power such privileges and still be a government, that matters would have to be settled by a fight sooner or later and that the winner would be the ruler of Bengal. The British won the battle of Buxar in 1764. But they still tried to enjoy all the privileges of their strength without taking on the huge task of ruling Bengal openly. It was only gradually over the next score of years that they came to admit openly that they were the rulers of millions of Indians.

One reason for this slowness was that these potentates were

The trial of Warren Hastings, impeached by members of the House of Commons and judged by the Lords, began in 1788 and did not end until 1795, after sittings totalling 145 days. This contemporary print shows the scene in Westminster Hall. It was a great public spectacle, and an admission ticket is reproduced right. Hastings was acquitted, but his expenses amounted to about £70,000.

in theory only a company of merchants. After all, they were only doing it for the money. Each one dreamed of becoming a 'nabob', as the very rich East India merchants were nicknamed, buying an estate in England and becoming a country gentleman, like the Pitt family who eventually produced two outstanding Prime Ministers. Few could reach such heights, but many could become very rich, especially if they were prepared to bully and cheat.

The Company, of course, was having to appoint more and more officials solely to govern Bengal, and these men too used their golden opportunities. Most of the huge population were very poor, prone to starvation and disease, while some were very wealthy. Besides paying taxes it was usual for people to give presents to officials of the nawab if they wanted favours – or even justice. The British took over this system, and used it mercilessly. One of the Company's officials reported in 1769:

'This fine Country, which flourished under the most despotic and arbitrary Government, is verging towards its Ruin while the English have really so great a share in its Administration . . . Their first consideration seems to have been the raising of as large sums from the Country as could be collected, to answer the pressing demands from home and to defray the large Expences here.'

That is not counting the corruption and unofficial extortion that was going on.

Warren Hastings, governor from 1772 to 1785, took on the task of cleaning out the corruption and setting up a strong and reasonably fair system of government. This is the beginning of a long and complicated story which cannot be included in this book, because his system was the foundation of the British Raj which eventually covered almost the entire subcontinent. Already the British Parliament was taking a lively interest in India, and the government was blamed for whatever went wrong, because it helped and partly controlled the East India Company. Both Clive and Hastings were accused in Parliament of taking bribes and ill-treating Indians. Considering the conditions the two men had been placed in, the charges were probably not fair, especially in Hastings' case, and the prosecutors may have been more interested in politics than justice. All the same, it meant that by the end of the eighteenth century it was accepted that what went on in India was the business of Great Britain and her responsibility.

BLOOD on THUNDER fording the RED SEA.

Two opposing views of the Hastings case, in contemporary cartoons. Above he is shown being carried by Lord Chancellor Thurlow, who presided at the trial, safely through the result of his crimes. Below he is shown as a noble patriot attacked by villainous politicians, who are recognizable as Edmund Burke, Lord North and Charles James Fox.

The POLITICAL BANDITTI assaulting the SAVIOUR of INDIA.

The struggle for North America

This was a land completely different from India. Here there were no ancient civilizations with great cities and teeming populations, but a wilderness of forests and mountains, long rivers and wide lakes, and a sparse population living mostly like Stone Age hunters. There was no trade in silk and cotton, gems, spices and tea. North America produced only furs and timber, though the land was good for farming when it had been cleared and in some areas tobacco could be grown on plantations. Compared to the East, it offered few attractions to merchants. But for anyone who wanted to settle there was space and a climate which Europeans found healthy.

By about 1740 thirteen colonies were firmly established by the eastern coast. All now were British, though some had been founded by Dutch or Swedes, and there were communities like the 'Pennsylvania Dutch' who were in fact Germans. Occupations varied, from the farming and fishing villages of the north to the great slave-operated estates of the south; however, despite the presence of the aristocratic plantation-owners and the wealthy merchants of towns like New York, it is probably true to say that most colonists were hard-working countryfolk who made a fair, though sometimes rough-and-ready, living. Religions, too, were mixed. Some colonies had been founded as refuges for Puritans, Catholics or Quakers, and what these people had in common was a tradition of refusing to accept that the government had the right to be obeyed in all things. In fact the British government had never bothered to take a tight grip on these colonies. Each colony was quite separate from the others, and had its own governor appointed from London,

Virginia was not only the oldest British colony in North America, but also the largest in population and in area during the eighteenth century. At this time Williamsburg was state capital, and every year from 1704 onwards the Assembly met in the Capitol building, shown here. The elected Burgesses met in the main room of one wing, and the nominated General Court (rather like a House of Lords) in the opposite wing. In the 1930s the little town, which had stagnated and decayed after it ceased to be the state capital at the end of the eighteenth century, was restored to its former appearance, and as Colonial Williamsburg attracts great numbers of visitors. The Capitol is almost entirely rebuilt, but carefully to its original design.

with an assembly of colonists to advise and assist in making local regulations and conducting the day-to-day business of the colony. Not only was Britain 3,000 miles away, but the Whig governments believed in interfering as little as possible with their subjects. So the colonists mainly lived as they chose.

On the western fringes, behind the trappers and Indian traders, settlers steadily moved forwards, turning the forests into fields. Away from the frontier there grew villages and towns which, despite a few variations which mark what has been classed as 'colonial architecture', looked very much like eighteenth-century villages and towns in north-western Europe. Though they could not yet match the wealth and culture of Lima and Mexico, the thirteen colonies contained many pleasant and prosperous places, and many cultivated ladies and gentlemen among their million-and-a-half inhabitants.

France's colonies were very different. Not only were they closely supervised by the government, but it seemed that they had to be, since too few Frenchmen were willing to settle into a new world. Farms fringed the St Lawrence River for short distances. This, the colony of Canada, had begun because of the hope that it marked the beginning of a waterway through America to the East. The only valuable trade, however, turned out to be the fur trade, which was carried on by the *coureurs*

Another distinguished Williamsburg building is the College of William and Mary (below), founded in 1693 and built in what is claimed to be the style of Sir Christopher Wren. The ordinary shops and houses may not have such proud associations, but, as the photograph above shows, their streets are pleasant, spacious and dignified.

above: *Savannah in 1734, the capital of General Oglethorpe's new colony of Georgia. The contemporary engraving shows it being laid out to a regular plan; there are four wards, each with a central square. The forest still hems it closely.*

below: *For the frontiersman, home was likely to be this. The picture is from a book published in 1826, but the material for it was collected thirty years earlier, and the picture can safely be taken to represent a typical log cabin.*

des bois, men who loved the hardships, dangers and adventures of their long quests through the endless forests.

Early in the eighteenth century France had founded another colony, Louisiana, near the mouth of the Mississippi. Already their explorers had penetrated along the great rivers which formed water highways through the wilderness, and soon soldiers were sent to build forts and blockhouses along them. By the 1740s the French colonies contained probably well under 100,000 colonists, but there was a chain of military posts linking Quebec with New Orleans. Sooner or later pioneers from the British colonies, moving westwards, must come up against this chain.

It is a sign of the contrast between North America and India that we have been able to explain all this without mentioning the natives of the land, the so-called American Indians. The reason, of course, is that they were on the whole so weak that European settlers could push them back from land they wanted, and slaughter them if there was much resistance. Since the French farmed so much less land, and since the *coureurs des bois* and soldiers did not interfere with their way of life, the Indians usually preferred the French.

As in India, the decisive struggle began when Britain and France were at peace. Here the two sides could not pretend that they were merely serving powerful native princes, but they could use an almost opposite argument — fights in the wild backwoods were one thing, full-scale war between civilized governments another. How far could this go without war? In 1753 the French governor, Duquesne, began to build forts in the Ohio region, which the British claimed. Some colonial militia led by the Virginian colonel George Washington tried to build and hold a fort there, but had to surrender. The British government now decided to send a strong force — it was still not war, because they were only trying to move trespassers, they said. The result was disastrous. General Braddock, marching against Fort Duquesne with a well-equipped force of 1,400 which included two regular regiments, was ambushed by a French force of 900, most of whom were Indians. Trying to fight in the forest as he had on European battlefields, Braddock lost half his men, three-quarters of his officers, and his own life.

Braddock's defeat was in 1755, and the next year the Seven Years' War officially began. Within four years the British were completely victorious in North America. Not only had some of their officers learned the lesson, but the Royal Navy was able

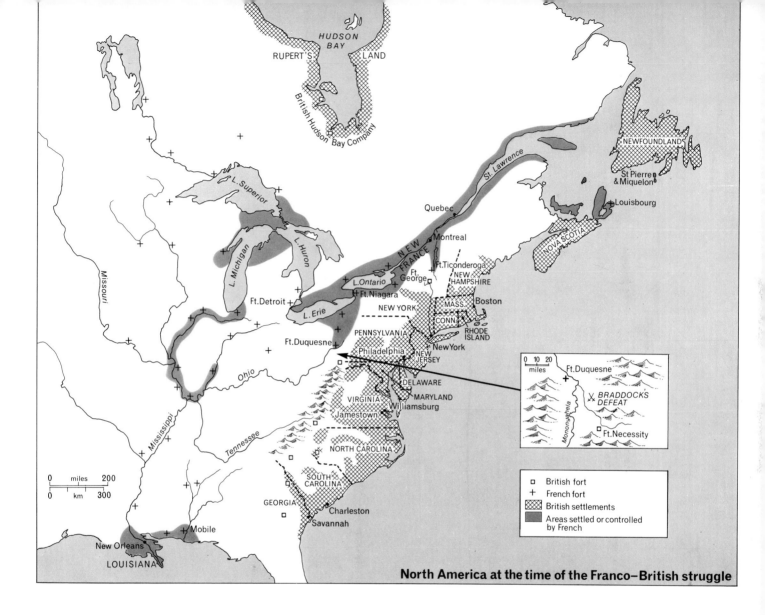

Inset map labels:

0 10 20
miles

Ft.Duquesne

BRADDOCK'S DEFEAT

Monongahela

Ft.Necessity

Legend:

□ British fort
+ French fort
▨ British settlements
▓ Areas settled or controlled by French

North America at the time of the Franco–British struggle

Map labels:

HUDSON BAY
RUPERT'S LAND
British Hudson Bay Company
NEWFOUNDLAND
St Pierre & Miquelon
Louisbourg
L. Superior
St. Lawrence
Quebec
NEW FRANCE
Montreal
Ft.Ticonderoga
NOVA SCOTIA
L. Michigan
L. Huron
Ft. George
NEW HAMPSHIRE
Missouri
L.Ontario
Ft.Niagara
MASS.
Boston
Ft.Detroit
L. Erie
NEW YORK
CONN.
RHODE ISLAND
PENNSYLVANIA
New York
Ft.Duquesne
Philadelphia
NEW JERSEY
Ohio
DELAWARE
MARYLAND
VIRGINIA
Williamsburg
Jamestown
Mississippi
Tennessee
NORTH CAROLINA
SOUTH CAROLINA
GEORGIA
Charleston
Savannah
Mobile
New Orleans
LOUISIANA

0 miles 200
0 km 300

to protect British convoys to America while preventing the French from being supplied and reinforced. Everyone has heard about how General Wolfe seized the Heights of Abraham and ensured the fall of Quebec, but not everybody realizes that the whole expedition depended on Admiral Saunders' ships. The year Quebec fell, 1759, was known as 'the year of victories'. Two of the others were at sea, Lagos and Quiberon Bay. Another was in Germany, at Minden, where an army paid by British money and including several British regiments smashed a French army which might otherwise have attacked Frederick the Great. William Pitt, the British Prime Minister who was responsible for the overall strategy, believed that by

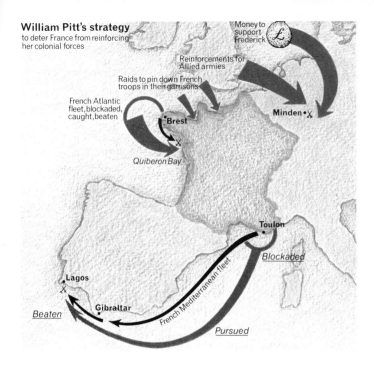

This coloured print is from a French book on American costumes published in 1796. The artist had probably never seen a 'savage Iroquois'; the Indian's leggings look far too tight and fashionable. But in general the information seems correct, including such details as the war-club (the original tomahawk) and the pipe with small hatchet blade (as supplied by white traders).

Sauvage Iroquois.

keeping the French busy in Europe he 'won Canada on the battlefields of Germany'.

In some ways this could be regarded as the first world war. The quarrels were between European powers, but the fighting spread round the world and decided the future of nations in Asia and America. The Peace of Paris, 1763, was the high point of the first British Empire. Among other gains, Britain got control of the whole of North America east of the Mississippi.

The Indians, of course, had no part in the peace terms, but some of them saw clearly what was going to happen. Without the French to oppose them, the British would steadily destroy the hunting grounds to make their farms and towns. As early as 1761 Pontiac, a chief of the Ottawas, saw that the Indians must combine now, while there was still time to get some French help. Many tribes were bitter enemies and few had much experience of working together with other tribes for any length of time. Nevertheless, Pontiac was so persuasive and the danger to the Indians so obvious that several tribes joined in a conspiracy to drive out the British.

The secret was well kept. When the attacks came in May 1763, though the two big forts of Detroit and Pitt (as Duquesne had been renamed) resisted, almost all the smaller western forts fell. At the same time, war parties struck at farms and settlements. For a few terrible weeks the whole frontier seemed to be collapsing in fire and blood.

In fact, Pontiac's rising was hopeless from the start. The French had already made peace, and could not give help. The Indians never penetrated the civilized parts of the colonies. If they had they might have spread terror, but they were too few to conquer, and their methods of warfare would have been as useless among towns and fields as Braddock's had been in the forest. Within weeks of the rising, British reinforcements were moving west, and Fort Pitt was relieved in early August. In the autumn many tribes made peace, and the whole thing was over by August 1764. Pontiac himself was murdered by another Indian five years later. Futile though it proved, his was the strongest attempt ever made to prevent the white man's progress from crushing the red man's way of life.

Pontiac was far too late. By 1763 the thirteen colonies were a group of prosperous little states which, taken together, were a match for much more formidable opponents than a few thousand despised savages.

A republic in America

The history of the United States of America is summarized in their flag. To know how each star was added is to understand the growth of that giant power. The stripes have remained unchanged since the beginning, thirteen for the original colonies which broke away from the British Empire. Why did they do it?

From arguments to bullets

In 1763 the British Empire might have seemed a good thing to belong to. It was prosperous and strong. The wealth from trade and the sailors who carried it would provide the money and men for invincible sea-power if war came. Yet, while able to protect her colonies, Britain was not despotic and did not interfere much. How, then, did some colonists come to think of George III and his ministers as tyrants?

Disputes arose mainly about money. The wars had been expensive, and the government thought it necessary to keep troops in America for fear of more trouble from Indians or perhaps French-Canadians. The colonies were not heavily taxed, and the government thought they should pay more; after all, the troops were for their defence.

So in 1765 Parliament passed the Stamp Act, which ordered that paper used for legal documents, licenses and newspapers must carry an official stamp, and this had to be paid for. At about the same time the government realized that it could get more money simply by enforcing the trade laws which already existed; colonial merchants were smuggling molasses (to make sugar and rum) from the West Indies — often from French islands — and so depriving the government of revenue.

To the surprise of the government, there was a furious reaction in the colonies. There were angry protests in the Virginia assembly, riots in Boston where the mob burned a store of the stamped paper, and a congress in New York with representatives from nine colonies to complain about the Stamp Tax. This last was most astonishing, as it had always been almost impossible to get the colonies to work together even for defence in time of war; each colony's assembly had normally said that it was up to the colony being attacked by French and Indians, with the British government, to look after

Colonel Henry Bouquet, 1719–65, a Swiss mercenary serving in the British army, proved outstandingly successful in dealing with the tribes of the Ohio country that had supported Pontiac. After beating them soundly, he negotiated peace. This engraving, from a book published in 1766, shows him making terms with Indians in 1764. He made them return their captives, but some small children had become attached to their Indian foster-parents and did not want to leave them.

its own defence. Now they were coming together to proclaim one simple belief:

'No Taxation without Representation!'

It meant that no British subject could be taxed unless his representative sat as a member in the Parliament which voted the tax. This was not a new idea – indeed, it had been partly responsible for the beginning of the English Parliament, simply because the king could not get money out of his richer subjects without their consent. Of course there were no colonial M.P.s at Westminster.

Was it really a quarrel over money after all? Or was it that many colonists resented being given orders of any sort from London, and that these people would always find something to protest about? There are very different opinions among historians, and you should make up your mind only after careful study of the events of the ten years that followed.

The government did not want trouble. In 1766 it repealed the Stamp Act and reduced customs duties so that the merchants could get molasses cheaply without smuggling. To save its dignity and to safeguard its legal rights, however, Parliament passed an act declaring that it had full powers over the whole British Empire.

Some colonists thought that the government had given way only out of weakness, and would try again. In 1767 new duties were imposed (on lead, glass, painters' colours, paper and tea) in such a way that the government thought that the colonists would agree that these were legal. But many objected, particularly in the colony of Massachusetts. In Boston it became common for mobs to jeer at the soldiers and attack any they caught alone. On 5 March 1770 the guard outside the custom house was attacked; they endured insults and stones, but when one of them was knocked down the soldiers opened fire. Five of the mob died. This was the 'Boston Massacre', as some colonists named it. Most colonists thought that the Bostonians had got what they had long been asking for, and a local court acquitted the soldiers of murder. But blood had been shed.

Also in March 1770 the government gave way again. It lifted the duty from everything except tea. Tea was retained as part of a scheme to help the East India Company, which at the time was in difficulties; the duty was so contrived that the colonists would pay less for their tea than people in Britain, and smuggling would hardly be worth while. Anti-government colonists had no intention of agreeing even to this. They wanted all true Americans to refuse to buy anything on which duty had been paid, no matter how cheap it was. On the night of 16 December 1773 a gang dressed as Indians boarded tea ships in Boston Harbour and threw the tea overboard. This was the 'Boston Tea Party'.

Boston again! The government would stand it no longer. It closed the port; without shipping, the town would soon be in poverty. At the same time, it withdrew the charter of the colony of Massachusetts; this abolished the assembly, so that the state could be ruled despotically. But some members of the former assembly met and called themselves a 'Provincial Congress'. They also organized colonists who were willing to come out with their guns if the government used troops; they claimed to be ready at a minute's notice, and were known as 'minute men'.

Everybody could see how dangerous the situation had grown. Representatives from all the colonial assemblies except Georgia's met in a congress at Philadelphia on 5 September 1774. Some thought that the government was right, but most feared that if the government succeeded in crushing Massachusetts, whether or not that colony had deserved it, then it might try to bully the other colonies. So the congress voted that the British Parliament had no right to raise taxes in the colonies, though it was able to impose duties for the purpose of regulating trade; and that the colonies should neither pay taxes nor trade with Britain until the government gave in. So it appeared that congress was not trying to find a way of ending the quarrel, but was declaring open opposition to the government. Boston was not alone.

It may seem that the story so far has not been very convincing, that the bickerings over stamps and tea were far too trivial to cause such a serious situation, even allowing for the way one thing can lead to another. The truth is that there were also other reasons why many colonists felt hostile to the British government. They resented the manners and attitude of British officers and officials, who sometimes made it very obvious that they despised most colonials as ignorant bumpkins. There was still a strong religious feeling among the Puritans of New England that the Church of England was no better than the Church of Rome, and they were horrified by the proposal to found an American bishopric among them. During part of the time when there was argument over customs duties and smuggling, trade was poor and the govern-

Part of a map of Boston and district, printed in 1775 when fighting had already broken out. It is plain to see why Boston was such a good harbour, and also how easy it would be to block it. The first big battle of the war was fought at Breeds Hill (12) — usually named after Bunker Hill (13) — when the British troops had to dislodge Americans who could have fired down upon the ships in the harbour.

ment got the blame. Finally, the government seemed to be favouring Catholic French-Canadians and even Red Indians rather than the colonists; the Quebec Act, 1774, guaranteed that the French-Canadians could keep their own laws and religion, and reserved for Canada that vast area between the Great Lakes and the Ohio from which settlers had been barred since the war but which many colonists had assumed would be opened up for them. All of these things helped to make many colonists believe that the British government would end by reducing them to servile obedience if they did not resist firmly.

Many British sympathized with the colonists. No less a person than William Pitt, then Earl of Chatham, thought that the government had handled matters badly, and tried to suggest compromises which would have the colonies helping in their own defence without actually being taxed. Others thought it was high time to deal firmly with the small number of self-seeking troublemakers and impudent ruffians who alone, they believed, were stirring up the colonies.

On 19 April 1775, troops were sent from Boston to seize a dump of arms which 'minute men' had stored at Concord. Armed farmers tried to stop them at Lexington. There was a small battle and the troops marched on to Concord to find that the arms had been destroyed. By now the whole countryside had risen. As the red-coated column marched back to Boston it was continually fired upon, and suffered many casualties.

Now that fighting had begun, the quarrel would not be settled until one side or the other admitted defeat.

The war for independence

The people who took up arms were not a united nation. They wanted to be free from outside interference in their lives, but what did 'outside' mean? Many a colonist regarded people from other colonies as outsiders. Besides, a very considerable number of colonists, perhaps half, remained loyal. It was obvious that those colonists who were prepared to fight the government must try to get some sort of union, some sort of agreed policy if they were to have any chance of resisting the redcoats.

In Philadelphia the congress met again on 10 May 1775. It declared itself to be the Continental Congress, thus assuming authority over all thirteen colonies. It set up the American Continental Army, and placed the former militia colonel, George Washington, in command. Then, as fighting spread and both sides became more determined, the Congress got rid

Lexington. The first shots of the war. This illustration by the well-known American printmaker Amos Doolittle, 1745–1832, shows a volley from the British regulars wreaking havoc among their untrained opponents. The pattern of this day was to be repeated throughout the war: the redcoats could usually win pitched battles, but could not hold down a hostile countryside.

of doubts and hesitations, and gave the rebels something definite to fight for. On 4 July 1776 Congress issued the Declaration of Independence with noble words of liberty for all.

No longer British rebels, but American patriots; the idea may have comforted Washington's men, but they needed more than this. Short of money and supplies, often disappointed, sometimes in hardship, frequently defeated, Washington's steadfastness was, nevertheless, turning the Continentals into something like an army, but it was a slow, hard task. Meanwhile, though American riflemen could inflict heavy casualties on British troops while sheltering behind trees and walls, they could not stand up to the discipline, bayonets and artillery of the redcoats in pitched battle. It was the same at sea. American sailors could worry the British with their raids, mostly against merchant ships, but could never seriously impede the Royal Navy. In America, besides the many loyalists in the thirteen colonies, both the French-Canadians and the Indians chose

to help the British, knowing well enough how much consideration they would receive from people like New England farmers. Britain was also able to enlarge her army by hiring several good regiments from the Prince of Hesse, in Germany.

Naturally the American patriots sought help. They received sympathy. Britain had beaten her foes and disappointed her allies too often to have any real friends. France particularly was only waiting for a change to avenge her defeats in the Seven Years' War, but she was not going to back a certain loser.

The decisive change was the surrender at Saratoga, 17 October 1777. Mainly because British commanders were too stupid or lazy to carry out their orders properly, a complete British army was cut off. The campaign which had been meant to drive a wedge between New England and the rest of the colonies, and so decide the war rapidly, had backfired. France declared war, and Spain followed. Next, some of the states of

The surrender at Saratoga; General Burgoyne hands his sword to General Gates. This painting by the American artist John Trumbull, 1756–1843, is not meant to be realistic, but a commemoration of a historic event with portraits of the leading Americans. The man in white buckskin is Daniel Morgan, a particularly able commander, who later won Cowpens, the only pitched battle that the Americans won against British regulars.

northern Europe, who had resented the way the British navy stopped and searched their ships in case they were carrying enemy goods, formed what they called the Armed Neutrality of the North. They threatened to fight if Britain interfered any more with their ships, and the Dutch did indeed use their guns.

Despite the strain, British forces in America continued to win most of the battles until in the autumn of 1781 an army was pinned against the coast by a much stronger force composed mainly of French troops. They should have been relieved from the sea, but at the critical moment French battleships were able to drive off the British. On 19 October, the second British army to surrender during the war did so at Yorktown. After this there was little fighting in America. Both sides held their positions and waited for peace. The British Parliament had come to see that, even if there were temporary successes, in the long run it would be impossible to hold down the thirteen colonies with so many of the colonists hostile.

Though Admiral Rodney smashed the French fleet in the West Indies at the Battle of the Saints, and General Elliott held Gibraltar in an epic siege, it was now just a matter for Britain to get out of the war as best she might. By the Peace of Versailles, 1783, Britain gave small colonial gains to France and Spain, and recognized fully the independence of the thirteen American colonies.

Making the Constitution

The patriots were citizens of a new and victorious state. Unfortunately, nobody was quite sure what that state was.

Take the very word 'state'. Normally it means a wholly independent country, often the home of a distinct and separate nation. In America, however, every one of the thirteen former colonies called itself a state. The key word must be 'united'. How strong was the union which bound those states together? Many Americans felt that they had fought to be independent, and this did not mean submitting to a Continental Congress sitting in Philadelphia.

During the war the patriots could be sure of one agreed aim: they had to win. As their famous writer and scientist Benjamin

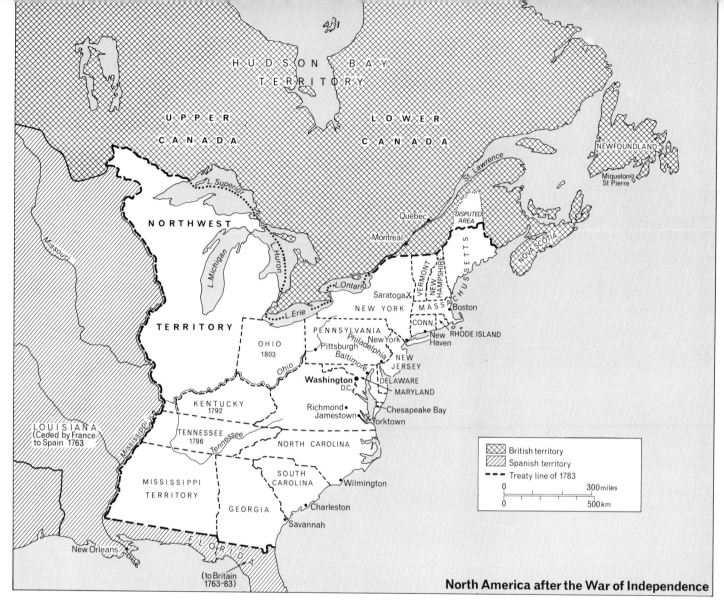

North America after the War of Independence

Franklin put it, they must 'hang together or be hanged separately'. But even then they were very bad at working together, as General Washington found whenever he tried to get supplies or even sensible regulations for his long-suffering troops. After the war the army was neglected, though it was practically the only thing which belonged to the thirteen states as a whole. Every state did as it pleased, coining its own money,

making its own laws, charging customs duties on merchandise from other states. Some states were even considering raising their own armies and navies, and signing their own treaties with foreign countries. The Americans were experiencing the old truth that it can be easier to win the war than to use the victory.

Danger was sharp and obvious. Rhode Island, to take one

This print by Amos Doolittle, dated 1790, shows the building from which the United States was first governed: Federal Hall, New York. On its colonial– classical style facade the stars, stripes and eagle are prominently displayed, and on the balcony George Washington is being sworn in as president.

notorious example, printed a great quantity of paper money which was in fact of no value, and then declared that her merchants could use this to pay their debts to people of other states. This sort of thing caused very bitter quarrels, and there would almost certainly be wars unless some rules could be applied soon.

In May 1787 almost all the states sent representatives to Philadelphia to try to agree on a constitution. Fortunately the lead was taken by educated men who shared Enlightened ideas. They agreed on a republic, with president and congress. They believed in Montesquieu's separation of the executive, legislative and judicial powers of government, so

the PRESIDENT would have full power to carry out the laws and direct the daily business of government;

the CONGRESS would have full power to make the laws;

and there would be a SUPREME COURT whose judges would have the final word about what was legal and what was not, even to the extent of being able to over-rule president or congress on points of law.

In view of the disputes that had taken place, it was vital to define very clearly what the government of the whole country could do, and what powers were left to the states. The central government would conduct relations with other countries, make alliances, peace and war; it would control the army, navy and postal services, issue money, fix weights and measures, charge customs duties. It could admit new states into the Union. Beyond that, however, every state had to look after its own people, making laws and punishing crime, for example, building roads and schools. The central government could not intervene unless there were serious trouble and the state government asked for help. To show that the central government was not tied to any one state, some land was set aside on the banks of the Potomac River, between Virginia and Maryland, and named the District of Columbia. This was where the capital would be built.

One awkward problem was how the states should appoint members to Congress. If members were elected so that each represented roughly an equal number of people, which seemed fair, then a few big states would dominate Congress, which seemed unfair to the smaller states. It seemed just as unfair to give each state, big or small, the same number of representatives. There must be a compromise. Congress was divided into two houses, like the British Parliament. The lower was called the House of Representatives, and representatives were elected according to the population of their states. The upper house was called the Senate, and every state — regardless of population — elected two senators. This solution did not satisfy everybody, but most thought it reasonable and it worked.

So the new nation was set up as a federation of states, and the central government was called the 'federal government'. Nobody could be sure whether an American's first loyalty was to state or federal government; but it could be hoped that if the Constitution were very carefully stated, there would be little chance of serious misunderstanding and dispute. It was written down and, after a great deal of argument, accepted by all the states. From then onwards the United States of America were to be held together by their written Constitution.

Like treaties, constitutions succeed only if people want them to succeed and are prepared for a little give-and-take to make them work. The leading American politicians were still very divided, especially between those who wanted a strong federal government and those who thought this would restrict liberty. Fortunately all were agreed that there was one man so widely respected and trusted that he was the only possible choice for president. He was George Washington, and even after two terms in office he had to insist on resigning. During those eight years from 1789 to 1797 he showed Americans that the Constitution could work well. Other men, cleverer than Washington, might have introduced all sorts of brilliant new ideas. He, wiser, knew that the Union needed a time of calm and steadiness, and these were exactly the qualities which he could bring to the task. Americans named the new capital after him, and called him the 'Father of His Country'; they were right to do so.

In Britain the name normally used is the War of American Independence. In America it is the Revolution. Which is nearer the truth? What does 'revolution' mean? Was American society transformed, or did people go on much as before, led by the same sort of men? Opinions differ, but there is no doubt about one thing: Americans claimed to stand for freedom, equality and justice; against despotism and privilege. Others admired the same ideals. In Britain, self-styled land of liberty, many had sympathized with American arguments even during the war. All over Europe, and especially in France, Enlightened people rejoiced at what they saw as a triumph of liberty and reason. Soon they were to see it nearer home.

THE SPIRIT OF THE UNION.

This print dates from 1860, when the United States seemed to be in danger of breaking up. (In fact there was a civil war from 1861 to 1865, but the Union survived.) By this time George Washington had become a legend and a symbol of the federal union. In the clouds behind the hero rises the new Capitol building in Washington D.C., still incomplete at the time.

4 THE GREAT FRENCH REVOLUTION

1789

On 30 April, in New York, George Washington was inaugurated as first president of the American republic.

On 5 May, in Versailles, the Estates General of France met. They were the nearest thing France had to Parliament or Congress, and this was their first session for 175 years.

The two events were connected. Not only had the success of the Americans encouraged the many Frenchmen of all classes who believed that despotic government should be a thing of the past, but the expenses of this last war against Britain had broken King Louis XVI's government financially. That was why the Estates General had been called at last.

The king had tried one finance minister after another, and all had been forced to the same conclusion. The only way to recover was to impose a new tax on land, and this time to make the nobles pay in full. But the nobles refused, though they knew how desperate the financial situation was. It was not that they just would not give up money or privileges. Some were thinking of how Louis XIV had reduced them to a class of pampered servants, and hoped that this was their chance to make the king recognize them once again as a real aristocracy, with the right to play a leading part in ruling the country. Some, too, agreed with the Enlightened writers that the state needed a thorough overhaul. There was also a feeling of exasperation at the clumsy, hesitating way the government behaved, getting itself further and further into a mess. In short, they were 'fed up'.

So were many other people, though sometimes for differing reasons. The *parlements* were powerful corporations of magistrates and lawyers, appeal courts which dominated the administration of justice in the various parts of France; they feared that their privileges were being threatened by Enlightened arguments – though they were themselves ready to use those same arguments if the government tried to use despotic methods against them. Bankers and merchants were worried by the government's inability to repay loans; and some of them had suffered humiliation at the hands of snobbish nobles, and would be glad of a chance to take revenge. Many peasants, too, resented the *corvée* (forced labour) that they had to do for the government and sometimes for their lord; the more prosperous peasants had another grudge, for even if they bought their land from the lord, as many of them had, they still had to go on paying feudal dues.

It sounds as though there was very widespread restlessness in France during the 1780s, though for different reasons which often had nothing to do with the government. It became worse after 1787 when bad harvests brought misery to very many of the poor. There was a feeling that something drastic *must* be done. Perhaps a strong, tough government could have ignored all this, and the feeling might have died away. In fact the king, bankrupt, well-meaning and weak, ordered elections to be held for the Estates General.

A cartoon of 1789 which represents a widely held belief of the time. The peasant carries the churchman and the noble, bowed beneath their weight; some of the taxes and other impositions are listed on the papers sticking out of their pockets. The peasant supports himself with his mattock, but birds and rabbits, protected to provide sport for the nobility, eat his seeds and crops.

There were three estates: Clergy, Nobles and the Third Estate, which stood for everybody else and in practice represented the middle class. Because it stood for so many, the king agreed that the Third Estate should have as many representatives as the other two combined. Excitement had heightened during the election period, and the 600 Third Estate representatives came to Versailles with *cahiers* (paper books) full of their electors' complaints, feeling determined to reform the whole system of government and to sweep away the privileges of the other two estates.

Immediately there was a dispute over procedure. How should the estates vote? Clergy and Nobles wanted each estate to vote separately, and its decision to be recorded simply as one voice; this, of course, meant that they would have two voices to the Third Estate's one, so any vote over their privileges was a foregone conclusion. The Third Estate argued that all the individual votes in all three estates should be counted; since a fair number of Clergy and Nobles sympathized with their ideas on reforms, this arrangement would ensure them a permanent advantage. So whoever won this preliminary argument would probably win every other important vote.

King Louis XVI hesitated, as he usually did. He was a kind man who wanted to please everybody, but was often persuaded by his family to support the Nobles. The Third Estate, in con-

trast, acted energetically. They declared themselves to be the National Assembly, speaking for all the French, and said that the representatives of Clergy and Nobles could join if they wished. Locked out of their meeting hall after making this revolutionary claim, they met in a tennis court on 20 June and swore not to disband until they had turned France into a constitutional monarchy.

A plan of the Bastille, redrawn from eighteenth-century plans, and a picture of the attack, drawn by a man who took part. While some of the attackers try to force the first drawbridge, soldiers who have joined the insurgents are firing their cannon at the defenders of the main building. Other attackers have made their way beyond the outer defences, and are also firing at the ramparts, with muskets. The picture is not the work of a skilled artist, but it is clear and vivid.

Dry ditch

Gardens

Second drawbridge

First drawbridge

Outer court

Moat

Approach from Rue Saint-Antoine

Governor's house

0   feet   200

0   metres   50

N

Again the king hesitated. Then he asked the Clergy and Nobles to join the National Assembly. The Third Estate had won.

It had been incredibly easy, so easy that people began to think there was something wrong. Was the king just playing for time? Was he sending for troops to march on Versailles and Paris? Rumours, suspicions, fears built up.

On 14 July the people of Paris stormed the Bastille.

Like many a famous event in history, it raises some difficult questions. Who were 'the people of Paris', for example? Solid middle-class shopkeepers, workmen desperate through unemployment and the shortage of bread, savage criminals from the slums – or a mixture of all sorts? Why did they rise? Did they really believe the stories that the Bastille was full of prisoners whose only fault had been to speak in favour of liberty, and that its guns were being prepared to bombard the city? Who invented and spread such tales? Who had something to gain from an uprising? Who organized and led it? Or was it unplanned, one of those things that explodes out of some trivial incident because everybody is so tense? There can be no simple sure answer.

But it was violent, dramatic. The story soon became a legend, a myth to inspire all who believed in liberty. The Bastille was seen as a great frowning stronghold of tyranny, and by destroying it the heroic people of Paris were promising freedom and justice to all Frenchmen. Had the other side won, it might have been dismissed as a foolish and brutal riot. As it is, 14 July has become a French national holiday.

Throughout France, violence erupted in towns and the countryside. Mobs murdered unpopular officials. Peasants broke into châteaux, mainly with the idea of burning the manorial papers which they thought to be the only evidence that entitled their lords to rents and services. Everywhere law and order seemed in danger of breaking down.

Now some nobles were convinced that France was ruined, that it was hopeless to stay and try to stop the rot. Led by one of the king's brothers, they 'emigrated' until France should, as they believed, return to sanity. Many of these *émigrés* settled just across the Rhine, at the courts of German princes, others just across the Channel, in Britain. Though they were only a small minority of nobles, some of them made it very obvious that they wanted to cause trouble and would never accept any reduction of their privileges.

In the National Assembly the reaction was quite different; not fear and anger, but a wave of renewed enthusiasm for sweeping away all those old customs which had become inappropriate and unjust. Many nobles shared this feeling, though some may only have been pretending, trying to make the best of a bad situation. So, on the night of 4 August, there was an amazing scene in the National Assembly. It began when a noble stood up and proposed the abolition of certain feudal privileges. Then another proposed some more, then another, and another, and the clergy joined in. They all seemed intoxicated with the joy of giving up rents, hunting rights, tithes, legal fees. Some observers cynically remarked that 'every man gave away that which he did not own', that nobles sacrificed church tithes and clergy offered hunting rights. Also, nobles were supposed to receive money compensation from their peasants for whatever they lost. Perhaps motives were mixed, and perhaps the scene on 4 August had been stage-managed, the start at any rate; but the result of that sensational night was the end of class privilege in France. Now all Frenchmen were free and equal before the law.

Why stop at Frenchmen? Had they any right to be treated

Another pro-revolutionary print, showing the scene in the National Assembly as the clergy and nobles gave up their privileges.

better than other men? The members of the National Assembly knew their Rousseau, and also the American Declaration of Independence (whose author, Thomas Jefferson, was at this time the American ambassador to France). After several August days full of fine words, the Assembly produced its Declaration of the Rights of Man, proclaiming the whole human race free and equal. Cool-headed people remarked that the declaration was confused and proposed nothing practical, but there were many who felt that this was the beginning of a wonderful new age of goodwill to all men.

Some of this optimism and enthusiasm was felt in other countries. 'Bliss was it in that dawn to be alive, But to be young was very heaven!' Wordsworth was a poet, and in love with a French girl at the time, but there were plenty of others who hoped soberly that if France were to become a constitutional monarchy like Britain, there would be a much better prospect of understanding and peace between the two countries which had so long been enemies. Meanwhile, the thought occurred to doubtless every practical politician in Europe that if France were to continue unsettled, she would soon be divided and powerless.

The constitutional monarchy

October 1789 saw another acute food shortage in Paris. The mob rose again. This time it marched to Versailles, burst into the National Assembly and the royal palace, and forced the king and his family to go back with them to Paris. As was becoming the custom, they bore in triumph a couple of heads on pikes – in this case guardsmen who had tried to keep them out of the palace. The National Assembly followed behind. Henceforth Paris was to be the home of the revolution.

Despite this sinister beginning, for many months it seemed as if the troubles were over. The mob faded away. There was more food about. The king seemed quite happy to agree with whatever the Assembly proposed, and on 14 July 1790 solemnly promised to accept the constitution which was being prepared. The power to make laws would belong to a new assembly, which accordingly was called the Legislative Assembly; the king would be able to veto a new law, but only for a limited

Pottery was nearly as popular as prints for illustrating topical events and ideas. These three plates reflect the constitutional monarchy. The nation is still under the crown and the royal lilies, the constitution covers all three estates and the clergy swear to maintain the constitution.

time. The Legislative Assembly was to be elected by taxpayers, which ensured that only men with some substance, even if small, had the vote. The poorest classes were not thought to be responsible enough. This was a middle-class Enlightened revolution so far.

Meanwhile all sorts of reforms were being enacted, making several sharp breaks with the past. The old provinces of France like Champagne and Gascony were abolished, and the country divided neatly and evenly into departments named after rivers and mountains like Marne and Jura. The nobility lost their titles and coats of arms. The lawyers' *parlements* were abolished, jury trial was begun, and the enormous task of sorting and codifying all the laws of France was taken in hand. Judicial torture was abolished; after some search for the most merciful way of executing criminals, the guillotine was adopted. A standard system of weights and measures was required, though it took eleven years before the metric system was finally introduced. (In 1793 the revolutionaries were even to invent their own calendar.) Everywhere the intention was to have order, reason, efficiency.

One institution had always aroused bitter criticism among

the Enlightened: the Church, they thought, was rich, useless, lazy, ignorant, corrupt. Further, it was international, and might take orders from outside France. Something had to be done quickly, anyway, because of a practical problem: since tithes and other church fees had been swept away, how were the priests to be paid? So the Assembly reorganized the Church thoroughly. It dissolved the orders of monks and friars except for those employed in teaching or nursing. It reorganized bishoprics and parishes as it had departments, and ordered that, instead of being appointed from above, bishops and priests would in future be elected. The government confiscated Church lands and undertook to pay the clergy like civil servants. Indeed, this was what all clergy must become; they must swear an oath accepting the authority of the government and in effect denying that of the Pope.

Probably this reform was only to be expected from men whose ideas had been formed by reading Voltaire and the rest, but it created serious difficulties. Half the priests and most of the bishops, including many members of the Assembly who had earned respect for their sincere support of the revolution until now, refused to take an oath which, to them, seemed to

left: *This* assignat *proclaims that it is backed by 'national domains', the land that the government has seized.*

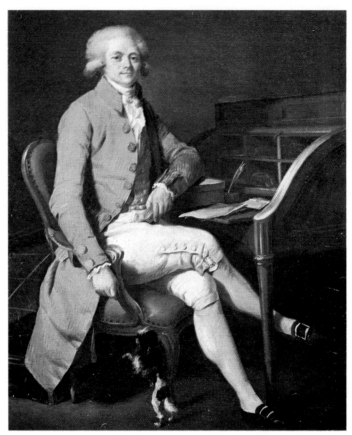

left: *This* assignat *proclaims that it is backed by 'national domains', the land that the government has seized.*

place the government above God. All over France ordinary people began to worry. Was the new government trying to improve religion, or was it really trying to get rid of it? Most of all the king, who had agreed to the other changes without much worry, was very distressed at being involved in this attack on the Church, and this may have changed his whole attitude to the revolution.

The government hoped that seizing Church lands might help them financially. (The stirring events of 1789 had done little to solve the financial problems which had partly brought them about.) The government was issuing paper notes called *assignats* instead of coins. It did not possess enough precious metal to guarantee the paper, but land was solid and valuable, it was argued, and therefore would do as well. In the event, far more paper money was issued than the land could possibly guarantee, people became suspicious and discontented, *assignats* lost value, and the government remained desperately poor.

The revolution moves on

Sometimes it is argued that all revolutions tend to take the same course, and that once a revolution starts there is no way of stopping it until it has passed through every stage to the end. It is worth considering whether or not this seems reasonable while studying the progress of this revolution in France.

Though many people had been upset about the Church, there had been no repetition of the violence of 1789. With goodwill and tolerance, the new constitution might work. But was there enough of that spirit?

It was all very exciting. For the first time ordinary Frenchmen had the chance to reshape entirely the French state. Eager, able young men talked, argued, planned. Naturally they formed clubs with others who shared their opinions, and soon these clubs resembled miniature political parties. Some were reasonably happy with the way things were going. Others wanted a system something like that of the United States, which would mean deposing the king. Others wanted a republic

Portraits of leading members of the three main republican parties. From right to left:

Manon Roland, wife of an inspector of manufactures; intellectual, idealistic and tactful; painted by J. E. Heinsius. Girondin.

Georges Danton, lawyer; passionately energetic, a dynamic orator; artist unknown. Cordelier.

Maximilien Robespierre, lawyer; cool, controlled but fanatical; painted by L. L. Bailly. Jacobin.

which was not federal but strongly held together by the central government; the most determined of these were the Cordelier and Jacobin clubs. In complete contrast were the royalists who wanted to restore the king's former powers.

With many different ideas in the air, all being pushed by groups of talkative, energetic people, there was not the tranquil, co-operative atmosphere needed to give the constitutional monarchy a fair chance. Besides, the people who had been poor and hungry in 1789 were still poor and hungry; now they were probably beginning to see that the constitutional monarchy was not going to make any difference to this, and many of them were ready for trouble. A very firm government might have been able to calm France, but the whole point about a constitutional monarchy is that it should not suppress the opinions of its subjects.

Then the king did something foolish. Worried about the Church, distrusting personally most of the leading politicians, afraid that his family was not safe in Paris, urged by his wife and her friends to act decisively, he agreed to flee secretly with his family and go to some regiments which he believed to be loyal to him. At first all went well, but at Varennes they were recognized and sent back under escort to Paris. After this, could any revolutionary trust the king?

Nevertheless things appeared to go on smoothly. The old Assembly ended on 30 September 1791, all of its members having unselfishly debarred themselves from being elected to the new. This was intended to bring in fresh vigorous members, but it also meant that the new Assembly lacked experienced men. This gave an opportunity to the leaders of the republican clubs, like Danton of the Cordeliers and Robespierre of the Jacobins, and especially a group of eloquent federalists known as the Girondins, after the district in south-west France where they originated. It did not matter that several of them did not actually have seats in the Assembly, nor that all the republican members together did not add up to a majority. These men were determined, clever, accustomed to speaking. Above all, these groups knew what they wanted. A small number of such people can often sway large numbers who are not so certain.

War

European governments were beginning to feel a little uneasy about France. It was all very well for that powerful kingdom to be weakened, but now it looked as though a king was actually in danger from revolutionaries. This sort of thing must be stopped before it could spread – and already French ideas were being eagerly discussed by some people in all the great cities of Europe. The Austrian royal family were particularly concerned because the queen of France, Marie Antoinette, had been an Austrian princess before her marriage. In August 1791 the Austrian emperor and the Prussian king met to discuss various international problems and at the end of it, pestered by *émigrés*, they issued a declaration that they might possibly intervene in French affairs provided that the other European powers agreed. This was intended to be a vague and cautious warning. It led to war.

In France, the reaction was naturally one of anger, as any people feel when outsiders try to interfere. But many parties welcomed the chance to have a war. Royalists expected that Frenchmen would rally, the army regain its loyalty, and that the king would return to power amidst victories and patriotic enthusiasm. (Anyway, if the army were to collapse, rotten with revolutionary ideas, the Austrians would restore the king to power – the royalists would win either way.) Republicans read the situation quite differently: the king – or, more likely, the queen – would be so obviously on the side of the enemy that this would finish the monarchy; meanwhile the French army, inspired by revolutionary enthusiasm and assisted by the revolutions which would surely break out in the enemy kingdoms, would sweep to splendid victories. Only a few, including Robespierre the Jacobin leader, thought it dangerous, arguing that a country at war needs a strong government, and that this could lead to some sort of dictatorship.

In Austria and Prussia, too, the pro-war politicians were gaining support, arguing that the French armies would quickly collapse. So both sides were willing to fight when in April 1792 the French government, then controlled by the Girondins, declared war.

Within a few weeks it was obvious which estimate of the quality of the French army had been right. It shrank back in a series of disgraceful defeats, and the Austrian and Prussian forces, without much exertion, moved slowly but steadily towards Paris.

The Terror and the Convention

In Paris there was panic and fury. People who had expected victory could think of only one possible explanation: 'We have been betrayed!' The town council, violently republican, took the lead. The royalists, unfortunately for them, could not deny that *émigrés* were marching with the invaders.

On 10 August a mob of Parisians and revolutionary soldiers attacked the palace of the Tuileries, where the king and his family were living. The guards, a regiment of Swiss professionals, did their duty, and soon their steady volleys hammered the attack to a standstill. But the royal family had fled for protection to the Assembly, where the king, horrified by the bloodshed, sent an order to the Swiss to cease fire and withdraw. They obeyed and were massacred by the mob.

The Assembly declared the king suspended, and imprisoned the royal family. But the Assembly itself was no longer in

The scene outside l'Abbaye Prison, Paris, in early September 1792, as shown in a contemporary print.

charge. In fact the Commune (town council) had taken over, with the members of the republican clubs. There was to be a National Convention to frame a new constitution, and this time all Frenchmen could vote.

By the beginning of September the prisons of Paris were full of alleged traitors awaiting trial. On the 2nd 'judges' apparently authorized by the Commune began to go round the prisons. Trials were quick, then prisoners were thrust out of the prison door and cut down by gangs waiting outside. The September Massacres went on until the 7th, and about 1,600 prisoners were butchered. It has been calculated that only about 150 people were involved in the actual killings; but nobody did anything to stop them.

On 21 September the Convention met, and immediately declared France a republic. At almost that moment the tide of war was turning. The day before, on the 20th, the Prussians had attacked the French army at Valmy, in a fog. The cannon fired. The Prussians marched forward. The French did not run away. The Prussians marched back again. The French treated this half-hearted encounter as a great victory, and they were right. Valmy saved France, and from this point the whole nature of the war changed. The French armies at last began to push forward, and Paris was saved.

The king was doomed. The Convention accused him of treason – he had indeed been in touch with the enemy – and found him guilty. He was sentenced to death by 361 votes to 360. On

above: *The Place Louis XV was a fine classical square, with a mounted statue of that king in the centre. It was renamed Place de la Révolution, and the guillotine was set up near the base of the destroyed statue. This contemporary print shows the scene at Louis XVI's execution. The square is now called Place de la Concorde.*

right: *Queen Marie Antoinette was taken to the guillotine on 16 October 1793, and the artist J. L. David, an enthusiastic revolutionary, made this sketch as she passed.*

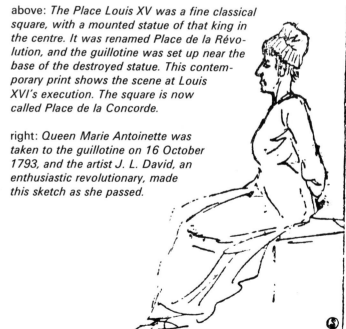

21 January 1793 he was taken to the guillotine which stood in what is now called the Place de la Concorde and beheaded. Though feeble as a king he had never lacked courage, and he died with dignity.

During that winter the full energy of the revolution began to

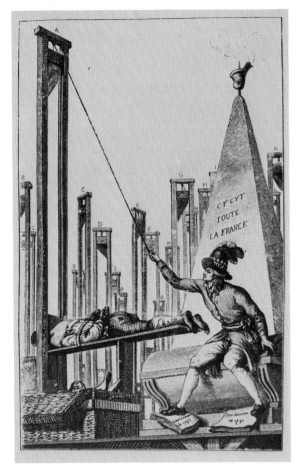

Two sides of the revolution's desperate struggle to win. The contemporary cartoon satirizes the Terror. Robespierre, seated on a tomb with the cap of Liberty impaled on its top and the inscription 'Here lies all France', is beheading his last possible victim, the executioner himself. The other print shows French grenadiers storming the Spanish fort of Rosas in 1795; their leader, pictured here in heroic posture, was rewarded by being made ambassador to Madrid after the peace treaty. This highly imaginative picture was not made until 1819, but it expresses the aggressive glory-seeking spirit which inspired the soldiers.

strike Europe. Recruits swelled the armies, many of them excitedly dedicated to victory for France and the revolution. New officers appeared, some of them daring, energetic and ambitious; now there was a chance that ability and success would be rewarded with high command. The new soldiers lacked the training to maneuver in well-disciplined eighteenth-century lines, so they were formed into solid columns which proved to have the courage and weight to charge through musketry and smash the enemy ranks. Waving their tricoloured flags and singing a new battle-song known as 'the Marseillaise', with melodramatic and bloodthirsty words, the armies of the revolution began to surge forward out of France, through the Austrian Netherlands and over the Rhine.

Other governments were alarmed, for it seemed that here was a force which was suddenly dangerously strong, directed by a government which did not respect the rules of eighteenth-century politics. For example, the French opened the Scheldt to all shipping when they entered the Austrian Netherlands, though it had been closed by international treaty (for the benefit of Dutch and British trade). For a mixture of reasons the Dutch, British and Spanish governments began to prepare for war. But the Convention did not shrink or hesitate – it declared war on the three of them on 1 February 1793.

Perhaps boldness was the only policy with any chance of success. The odds were heavy, and more troops were needed. There were not enough volunteers now. Conscription was ordered. But not all Frenchmen were revolutionaries. Many by now loathed the revolutionaries for some of the things they had done. If they were going to be forced to fight anyhow, then they would much rather fight against the revolutionaries than for them. Risings broke out in many places, especially the west. It has been said without too much exaggeration that soon Paris and a quarter of France were fighting Europe and three-quarters of France.

In this crisis the Convention, on 6 April 1793, set up a nine-man committee and gave it dictatorial powers. It was named the Committee of Public Safety and it decided to achieve unity and loyalty through terror. Not only royalists, but revolutionaries whose ideas did not seem completely reliable, would be exterminated for the good of France and the revolution.

The first revolutionaries to go were the Girondins. Their federal ideas meant a weak government, and must be opposed to the Committee of Public Safety. Then General Dumouriez, a friend of theirs, was defeated by the Austrians and deserted to the enemy; so the Girondins must obviously be traitors! The leading Girondins were arrested in June, guillotined in October. The revolution had begun to 'eat its own children'.

The Reign of Terror lasted from summer 1793 to autumn 1794. The details of the story are complicated but the main features are terribly and astonishingly clear. In Paris it became a life-and-death power struggle among the leaders of differing groups. Danton seemed to be master, but in April 1794 he and his friends were guillotined by Robespierre. The executions increased still more. Then, late in July 1794, Robespierre and his Jacobins were themselves overthrown and guillotined by members of the Convention terrified that it might be their turn next. After Robespierre, executions became fewer.

Outside Paris the Terror meant merciless punishment for rebels. When the Convention's commissioners put down the rebellion at Lyons, they mowed down their prisoners with cannon. At Nantes they packed them into barges and sank the barges, slowly. By such means, with the guillotine and much hard fighting, the rebellions were stamped out by early 1794.

There was success against foreign enemies, too. Not only were the new conscript armies becoming more skilled, but – though often unpaid, ragged and hungry, for the revolutionary governments were chronically short of money – they were high-spirited and daring. The new officers, too, were taking their chances, and some of those who got to the top were brilliant.

The revolution under attack 1792–3

It is important to remember, too, that the Committee of Public Safety was not merely a gang of terrorists: some members, particularly an engineer officer named Carnot, worked hard and well to provide the organization and support without which the armies could not even have existed.

Early in 1795 the Netherlands were conquered. France absorbed all the land on her side of the Rhine into the French Republic, and created from the remaining provinces the Batavian Republic. This was the first of the revolutionary 'satellites'. In May Prussia made peace, leaving France a free hand on the German west bank of the Rhine. In June Spain made peace, giving France a West Indian colony, Santo Domingo.

By October 1795 it was clear that the revolution had weathered the storm. The Convention had only been intended as a temporary assembly, to retire after it had worked out a new permanent constitution for France. Now it did so. The new constitution was disliked by many parties, royalist and republican alike, and the mob of Paris rose. This time the mob was swept away by the guns of the revolutionary army. In some ways this was the most significant battle yet.

73

On 13 Vendémiaire, Year 4 (5 October 1795, by the pre-revolutionary calendar) the revolution ended, according to one way of thinking. On that day the cannon and disciplined volleys of the troops smashed the power of the Paris mobs, and the Directory was secured. This contemporary engraving shows the fighting at the church of St Roch; some civilians are fighting on the same side as the soldiers to drive the rebels away from the church.

The Directory

The new government has the reputation of having been probably the most rotten that France has ever known. Partly, perhaps, it was the reaction after the Terror. Many Parisians were interested in making money and having a good time, and in nothing else. The government thought the same.

At the head were five Directors, who held the executive power under the new constitution. The legislative power belonged to the Council of Elders and the Council of 500; once again the vote was restricted to taxpayers, and this time it was decreed that two-thirds of the members of the old Convention must have seats in the new Councils. These men wanted to keep their jobs. They took bribes, swindled, double-crossed. If, in spite of all, elections still went against them, they declared the results mistaken and arrested their opponents. It is true that there were some honest men, like Carnot, 'the organizer of victory', in the Directory and its Councils; that France was

suffering all the after-effects of foreign war, civil war, terror and near-famine, and that no government could have cured all this; and that the Directory did carry on the war with success. But these cannot excuse the corruption.

The success in war was mainly the work of one man, a little Corsican officer who was Italian in looks, accent and name: Napoleone Buonaparte. It was he who had routed the mob in October 1795, and he was given command of an army partly as a reward for this, partly because he had married the ex-mistress of the most powerful Director, and partly because he seemed to have ideas and energy. The army which the twenty-six-year-old general took over was facing the Austrians and their Piedmontese allies on the borders of northern Italy. The French were not doing well here, while on their other front, where they were facing Austrian armies in Germany, the French were being driven back. The new general changed everything in a brilliant campaign, full of bold and unexpected moves. Against heavy odds he became master of Italy and compelled Austria to ask for peace.

In early 1798 revolutionary France had not only extended

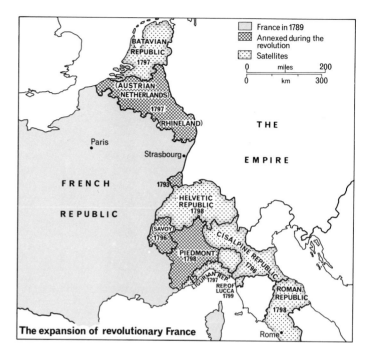

The expansion of revolutionary France

France in 1789
Annexed during the revolution
Satellites

above: General Bonaparte in 1798, engraved from a painting by J. Guérin.

right: Under the Directory some fashions went wild. The women who affected such styles were called merveilleuses, *marvellous, and the men* incroyables, *incredible. This picture is dated 1796, though it comes from a series intended to depict France in 1797.*

LES MERVEILLEUSES

her own frontiers, but had created more satellites in Switzerland and Italy. Some people welcomed the French troops as liberators, others detested them as robbers; doubtless many adjusted their views in the light of experience. Whatever they thought, France seemed triumphant.

Only Britain remained at war. The Royal Navy held the seas and had defeated every attempt to shake its grip. There seemed no way of getting a French army into Britain. With French encouragement there had been a serious revolt in Ireland in 1798, but France had failed to get much help to the rebels and they had been crushed. General Bonaparte (he now spelled his name in a French fashion) was invited to organize an invasion of Britain but, knowing the risks, declined. Instead he persuaded the Directory to let him strike eastwards, in the direction of the supposed source of Britain's riches, India. The first step would be to seize Egypt as a base.

General Bonaparte's expedition reached Egypt safely; the British navy had withdrawn from the Mediterranean after the defeat of Austria and now a fleet under Rear-Admiral Nelson, sent specially to intercept Bonaparte, failed to find him. Near the Pyramids he fought the Mamelukes, splendid horsemen who ruled Egypt under the Sultan of Turkey; he shot them to pieces and became master of Egypt. But less than two weeks later, on the night of 1 August 1978, Nelson's fleet found its target and sailed into Aboukir Bay, in the delta of the Nile, where the French warships were anchored, and destroyed Bonaparte's fleet. He was trapped in his conquest. He decided to march on Constantinople and conquer the Turkish Empire. He might have done it, too, but once again sea-power stopped him. The British navy captured his heavy guns as he was having them ferried along the coast, and then helped the Turks to beat him back from the walls of Acre. He had to retreat to Egypt.

The opening of the battle of the Nile, as painted in 1800 by the British marine artist N. Pocock. The French line-of-battle ships are anchored like a wall across the bay, with their frigates sheltering behind. But the British have guessed that it is just possible to sail round one end, and so they can bring all their strength against a few of the immobile French ships at a time.

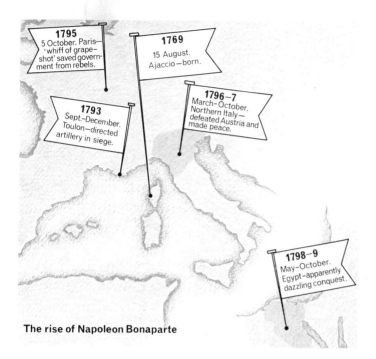

1795
5 October. Paris—
'whiff of grape-
shot' saved govern-
ment from rebels.

1769
15 August.
Ajaccio—born.

1793
Sept.–December.
Toulon—directed
artillery in siege.

1796–7
March–October.
Northern Italy—
defeated Austria and
made peace.

1798–9
May–October.
Egypt—apparently
dazzling conquest.

The rise of Napoleon Bonaparte

In France most people did not realize the true position. They understood only the conquest, and thought that the hero of Italy was now bringing the gorgeous East beneath the sway of France. But they could see clearly enough how badly things were going everywhere else. A new Tsar (unbalanced, like an earlier one) had changed Russian policy and entered the war on Britain's side. Austria, encouraged, renewed the fight. Though a British–Russian expedition in the Netherlands had failed miserably, a Russian–Austrian campaign in Germany and Italy was a great success. The last effective French forces had retreated into Switzerland, and the outlook was grim. Inside France things seemed to be slipping from bad to worse. Poverty and discontent seemed sharper, brigands had increased enormously, and no traveller felt safe unless he was well armed and escorted.

At this moment the hero came to the rescue. General Bonaparte returned from his Eastern triumphs to help the hard-pressed people of France. (The truth was that he had abandoned his army trapped in Egypt, and that his frigate had been lucky to slip past patrolling British warships.) By sheer luck the news of his return coincided with news of French successes

Napoleon Bonaparte could not allow it to be thought that he had ever failed. He always treated the Egyptian expedition as a glorious triumph of his military genius and a brilliant demonstration of his encouragement of learning. These are pieces from a Sèvres dinner service made for him in 1811, with decorations based on the drawings of the scholars and artists he had taken to Egypt with his army.

Bonaparte and the Council of 500, according to a pro-Bonaparte print; the faithful grenadiers protect their general from the daggers of his enemies. In fact it is hard to tell how serious the threats were. The daggers were part of the official costume of the 500; like the pseudo-togas, they reflected the fashion for admiring the virtues of ancient republican Romans like Brutus. Right, the same incident as the English cartoonist Gillray saw it.

EXIT LIBERTÉ a la FRANÇOIS! — or — BUONAPARTE closing the Farce of Egalité at St Cloud near Paris Nov.r 10.th 1799.

in the Netherlands and Switzerland. Then the Russians blamed their allies for not helping them sufficiently, and went home in a huff. Everything seemed to be giving General Bonaparte his big chance. Some of the Directors came to an agreement with him, and they planned secretly.

On 9 November 1799 they suddenly seized power – the sort of take-over backed by the threat of force which is called by its French name, *coup d'état*. When, next day, the Council of 500 refused to accept Bonaparte as their ruler, grenadiers with fixed bayonets pushed them out of the hall.

The Consulate

There was yet another constitution. This time the legislature was divided into three houses: a Senate of 80 members, a Tribunate of 100, a Legislative Chamber of 300. Their powers were limited and they were appointed by a complicated and indirect process which gave little control to the ordinary voters. The executive, which held the extra power the legislature had lost, consisted of only three men, the Consuls, and the First Consul had much more authority than the other two. The effect of all this was that France was ruled by the First Consul alone; his name was Napoleon Bonaparte.

It is sometimes said that revolutions always end with the rule of one strong military man, a Caesar or a Cromwell. If we try to explain this, it may be that after years of disorder and fear people yearn most for a strong government that will protect them; safety seems more important than liberty. The First Consul held a plebiscite; that is, all the voters were asked if they wanted the new system or not. The result was 3,011,107 for the Consulate, 1,567 against.

Did Napoleon give the French people what they wanted after a decade of upheaval? He organized the whole country under Prefects, one to each department. He had the coding of laws, begun under the constitutional monarchy, completed and the result issued as the Code Napoleon. He organized a more efficient system of taxation. He had roads and harbours built and improved. He made a *concordat* or agreement with the Pope which ended the revolutionaries' feud with the Church. He replanned the whole educational system, from elementary school to university. According to his admirers, he gave the French people the benefits of the revolution without the drawbacks. The revolution was accomplished.

Even for Bonaparte, who was extremely quick at getting results, this amount of work took several years. Meanwhile, he brought victory and peace. After a spectacular march across the Alps in May 1800 he defeated the Austrian army in Italy at the battle of Marengo. The other main Austrian army, in Germany, was beaten in December at Hohenlinden, and Austria sued for peace in 1801. Only Britain continued to fight, safe behind her navy but unable to do serious damage to France. At last both sides recognized that further fighting was pointless. On 27 March 1802 the Peace of Amiens was signed between Britain and France. The revolutionary wars were over.

The First Consul crossing the Alps, as imagined by J. L. David, who had now become an ardent Bonapartist. Many of David's paintings were certainly propaganda, but they were also sincere in their admiration for Napoleon.

5 NAPOLEON'S EUROPE

When we want a word to describe a bold and brilliant action we sometimes use 'Napoleonic'. This has little to do with Napoleon Bonaparte's government of France, but much to do with his reputation as the greatest military genius in modern history.

There is tremendous excitement in the Napoleonic epic. For ten years his armies were almost constantly on the march, conquering from one end of Europe to the other. Warfare has rarely looked so fascinating – splendid uniforms, spectacular charges, dramatic triumphs and disasters, heroic leaders and valiant soldiers, and the whole great game played by captains of the highest intelligence. For France it was a time of un-equalled glory, when all Europe obeyed her leader.

The other side was there too, the suffering of war, the heed-less brutality and deliberate cruelty. There was nothing roman-tic about being mangled with grapeshot, slowly dying of grangrene or frostbite or fever. Prisoners often rotted in foul conditions, as on the notorious British hulks. Even for the lucky ones war meant heat and cold, dust and dirt, exhaustion and hunger.

Such were the glory and misery thrust on the young men of Europe. They had no choice. Despots – and the constitutional governments of Britain likewise – had long 'pressed' men by various means to serve in the army or navy or militia. The French revolutionaries, in the desperate days of '93, had used conscription on a great scale. Now almost every government in Europe felt that it had to swell its armies by the same means. The well-drilled professionals of the eighteenth century were being replaced by massive hosts of half-trained conscripts.

For good or ill, was it Napoleon himself who caused the wars? He seems to have had a mind which thought naturally in military terms. One reason why he was able to restore order and peace within France was that he organized the country as he would an army, with clear orders and discipline. He was ambitious, and he never shrank from spending other men's lives. But the governments of other countries were very ready to continue and renew their struggle against what they saw as the French menace, and they too must share the responsibility for the glories and miseries.

left: *The colour and excitement of war, expressed by the British military artist Denis Dighton, 1792–1827. Though he often showed soldiers realistically, here the artist has shown them in full parade uniform which would rarely have been seen in the mud and dust of active service. While from a hill in the background the Royal Horse Artillery are firing their guns and high officers look on, the 14th Light Dragoons meet the French hussars in headlong charge. The date is probably 1813, the year when the 14th captured what must be one of the strangest regimental trophies; pursuing the French after Wellington's victory at Vitoria in northern Spain, they carried off Joseph Bonaparte's silver chamber-pot.*

right: *The brutality and pathos of war seemed more real to the Spanish artist Francisco de Goya, 1746–1828. Between 1810 and 1813 he made a series of eighty-three etchings entitled 'The Disasters of the War'. These are two of them. The upper picture shows infuriated peasants slaughtering French soldiers. The lower shows the plight of a child whose mother has fallen victim to the hardships of war.*

The years of triumph

It started with Britain. Most historians think that the Peace of Amiens was doomed from the start. Neither side trusted the other, and both were right. When it came to carrying out some of the terms of the treaty which would involve the loss of military advantages, Britain refused to leave Malta (which her navy had 'liberated' from its French invaders in 1799 and found to be a valuable base) and France would not evacuate Switzerland. War was renewed in May 1803.

Meanwhile Napoleon was showing how ambitious he was. In August 1802 he became First Consul for life, with the right to appoint his successor. In May 1804 he was proclaimed Emperor of the French. The French were willing enough; the plebiscite on this latest change in the constitution showed 3,572,329 for, 2,569 against. The Emperor lost no time in creating a glittering court. While Consul, he had founded the Legion of Honour, allowing people who had done distinguished work to wear a ribbon on their coats. Now he set up a whole new nobility. Outstanding generals became Marshals of the Empire. Many got titles – Prince, Duke, Count – and so did ministers and high officials. Dazzling uniforms went with high offices. Had the pendulum swung right back? At least the new nobles on the whole had earned their positions and the new monarchy was more efficient than the old.

You may have noticed how many Roman names and ideas the French used about this time. During the revolution some politicians thought they were reviving the republican virtues of such heroes as Brutus, Cincinnatus, the Gracchi. Napoleon followed suit: Emperor not King, a laurel wreath instead of a crown. His regiments still bore the revolutionary tricolour, but now topped by a gilded eagle. In their own way, the revolutionaries and Napoleon were following the 'classical' traditions of the eighteenth century, and this extended even to furniture design and ladies' fashions.

Though these French fashions spread among the wealthy classes all over Europe, this did not mean admiration for the new rulers of France. The kings and gentlemen of Europe felt that they belonged with the sort of people who had ruled France before 1789, the old regime as it came to be known. They sneered at 'the Corsican upstart' and were furious when he and his new 'aristocrats' gave themselves the same airs as

The Emperor Napoleon in his coronation robes, painted in 1806 by J. A. D. Ingres, an artist who particularly admired classical styles.

A fashionable gathering at the Café Frascati, Paris, in 1807, depicted by P. L. Débucourt, and the famous literary and political hostess Madame Récamier, 1777–1849, portrayed by David. Both paintings show the Empire style in fashions and furnishings, with its strong classical influence.

themselves. This may have been one reason why the rulers of Britain were not impressed by a letter addressed by Napoleon on 8 January 1805 to King George III: 'Monsieur my Brother; called to the throne of France by Providence, and by the votes of the Senate, the people and the army, my first impulse is to pray for peace.' The letter, written only five weeks after Napoleon's coronation, argued that without peace Britain and France could go on struggling for centuries, so difficult was it for one to overcome the other. His overture was ignored.

The British government thought that France could be

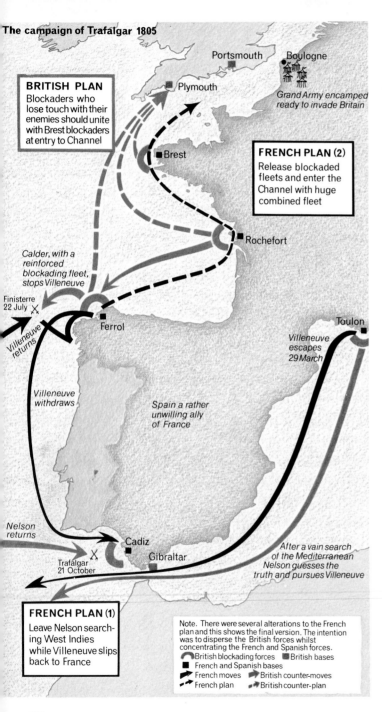

The campaign of Trafalgar 1805

Portsmouth
Boulogne

Plymouth

Grand Army encamped ready to invade Britain

BRITISH PLAN
Blockaders who lose touch with their enemies should unite with Brest blockaders at entry to Channel

Brest

FRENCH PLAN (2)
Release blockaded fleets and enter the Channel with huge combined fleet

Rochefort

Calder, with a reinforced blockading fleet, stops Villeneuve

Finisterre
22 July

Villeneuve returns

Ferrol

Toulon

Villeneuve escapes 29 March

Villeneuve withdraws

Spain a rather unwilling ally of France

Nelson returns

Cadiz

Gibraltar

After a vain search of the Mediterranean Nelson guesses the truth and pursues Villeneuve

Trafalgar
21 October

FRENCH PLAN (1)
Leave Nelson searching West Indies while Villeneuve slips back to France

Note. There were several alterations to the French plan and this shows the final version. The intention was to disperse the British forces whilst concentrating the French and Spanish forces.
British blocking forces ■ British bases
■ French and Spanish bases
➤ French moves ➤ British counter-moves
┅➤ French plan ┅➤ British counter-plan

84

overthrown, even if not by Britain alone. Once again the Prime Minister, William Pitt (younger son of the earlier Prime Minister who had become Earl of Chatham) kept trying to form alliances or coalitions against France. What is known as the First Coalition had been in 1793 (page 72), and 1799 (page 77) had seen the Second. Now the Third Coalition looked like being the strongest yet, because Austria and Russia were joining Britain, and they knew now what sort of a task they were taking on. They were determined to use their combined strength properly to crush France this time.

Napoleon, too, whatever he may have said in his letter, had hopes of crushing Britain. Once he had a French army in England, he was convinced, the British forces would soon be destroyed. The problem was to get the army across the Channel. His first step was to persuade the Spanish government to assist him, so that he would be able to use their navy. This, he thought, would give him such a numerical superiority in battleships that he would be able to clear the Channel of the British navy, certainly for long enough to get his army across safely. The problem was to bring enough of his ships together, because the French and Spanish naval bases were constantly watched by British ships. Napoleon, as the sketch-map shows, produced a plan. On paper, it should have had a good chance of success, but it failed partly because the British commanders had made plans themselves which would parry such an attempt, and partly because of the unpredictable conditions of warfare at sea which Napoleon never sufficiently took into account. The result was the battle of Trafalgar and the destruction of the main Franco-Spanish fleet. (Typically, Napoleon cast all the blame on his admiral, who then committed suicide.)

Well before Trafalgar Napoleon had realized that his naval plans had failed, and marched his great army away from its camp on the cliffs of Boulogne, facing England. In a swift, brilliantly organized march he struck across Germany, and surrounded and captured 20,000 Austrian troops at Ulm on the Danube, on 17 October 1805, four days before Trafalgar. He swept on, through Vienna, and met the Russian and Austrian emperors with their main armies at Austerlitz on 2 December.

The battle of the three emperors was the greatest victory of Napoleon's career. With 65,000 men he routed 80,000; but Napoleon saw to it that he had more troops than the enemy *in*

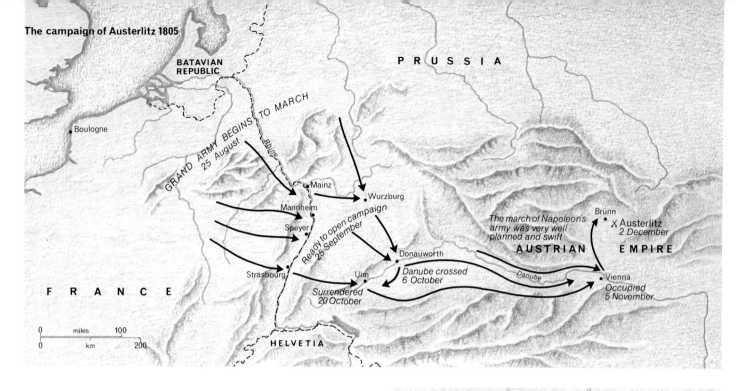

The campaign of Austerlitz 1805

the key positions at the right time. It was said by another great commander, Wellington, that Napoleon's presence on a battle-field was worth 40,000 men, and certainly this would seem to have been true at Austerlitz. The Tsar retreated and the Austrian emperor had to beg for peace.

Now, incredibly, Prussia declared war. Napoleon had be-haved in a very high-handed manner in Germany, and Prussia had good reason to be annoyed, but the Prussian government must have been completely blind to the strength of the French and must have thought that they still had Frederick II and his army with them. On 14 October 1806, at the twin battles of Jena and Auerstadt, the famous Prussian army was shattered and the French overran almost the whole kingdom.

Now only the Russians remained. In February 1807 neither side could claim victory after a bloody hammering-match at Eylau, but in June at Friedland the Russian army was beaten and the Tsar decided to make peace.

Napoleon had not destroyed Russian strength, but he did better. He conquered the Tsar personally. The two emperors met on a raft on the River Niemen at Tilsit, because this was

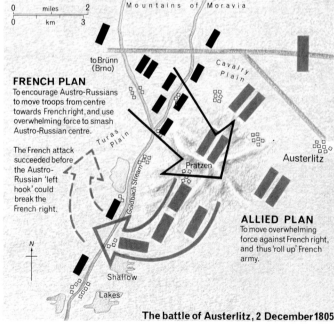

FRENCH PLAN
To encourage Austro-Russians to move troops from centre towards French right, and use overwhelming force to smash Austro-Russian centre.

The French attack succeeded before the Austro-Russian 'left hook' could break the French right.

ALLIED PLAN
To move overwhelming force against French right, and thus 'roll up' French army.

The battle of Austerlitz, 2 December 1805

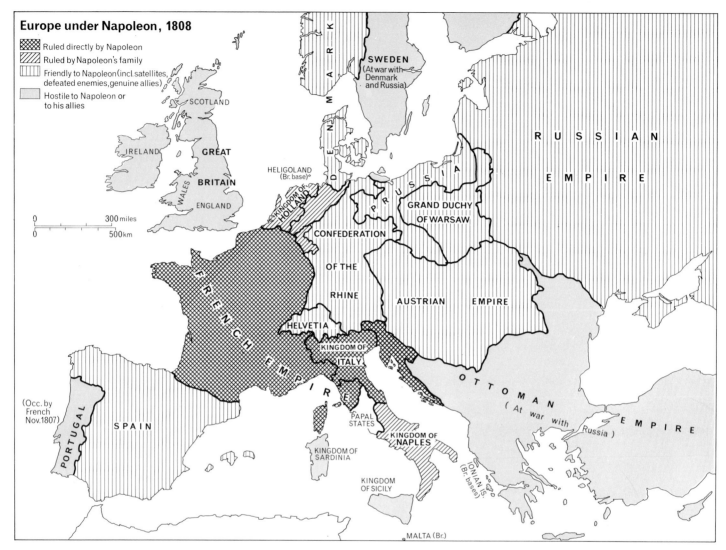

Europe under Napoleon, 1808

- Ruled directly by Napoleon
- Ruled by Napoleon's family
- Friendly to Napoleon (incl. satellites, defeated enemies, genuine allies)
- Hostile to Napoleon or to his allies

SCOTLAND

IRELAND

GREAT

BRITAIN

WALES

ENGLAND

HELIGOLAND
(Br. base)

0   300 miles
0   500 km

SWEDEN
(At war with
Denmark
and Russia)

DENMARK

PRUSSIA

RUSSIAN

EMPIRE

KINGDOM OF HOLLAND

GRAND DUCHY
OF WARSAW

CONFEDERATION

OF THE

RHINE

AUSTRIAN   EMPIRE

FRENCH EMPIRE

HELVETIA

KINGDOM OF
ITALY

(Occ. by
French
Nov. 1807)

PORTUGAL

SPAIN

PAPAL
STATES

KINGDOM OF
NAPLES

OTTOMAN

(At war with   Russia)

EMPIRE

KINGDOM OF
SARDINIA

IONIAN IS.
(Br. bases)

KINGDOM
OF SICILY

MALTA (Br.)

undeniably neutral and easy to keep strictly private. (Here they were mistaken – a spy in British pay quickly reported the details of their meeting to London.) Tsar Alexander I was a young and idealistic man. Napoleon had enormous powers of persuasion and charm when he wished; all who met him admitted this, and few could hold out against his spell. By the end of the meeting Alexander was not merely Napoleon's friend, but his devoted disciple, willing to share in making a new and better Europe, as designed by Napoleon.

The map and its information will explain the new shape which Napoleon gave to Europe. Was it truly better for the people who lived there?

For some, it meant living under a much fairer and more efficient government and under laws which treated everyone equally instead of favouring nobles and clergy. It meant that people in central Europe were more free to travel and trade without having to cross the innumerable frontiers of tiny principalities. The whole arrangement seemed more simple and sensible. Habits and restrictions which had grown old and often obsolete over a thousand years were scrapped. To that extent Napoleon was spreading the revolution abroad.

Not everybody approved. He was not 'Jacobin' enough to destroy the old nobility, and indeed he encouraged the *émigrés* to return to France, but he did make them less important. Naturally, many of them were annoyed. Ordinary people were sometimes just as disgruntled. They saw the French as foreigners throwing their weight about. They marched all over, seizing whatever they wanted; Napoleon in fact thought it usually quicker and cheaper for an army to 'live off the country', so his troops naturally became expert pillagers. To add insult, some of them seemed to think that they were a superior nation conferring benefits on inferiors. Then Napoleon expected all his friends in Europe to help him in his wars. It would take some time for the new Europe to settle down.

The 'nation of shopkeepers' and the 'Spanish ulcer'

Britain was alone again, but her navy seemed as invincible as ever. No ship could safely sail the high seas around Europe without the British government's permission. Despite the efforts of blockade-runners, this meant in effect that nobody in Napoleon's Europe could obtain overseas goods unless the British chose to supply them, at whatever prices they saw fit to ask.

How could Napoleon damage Britain? The British were, he said, borrowing a phrase from their own economist Adam Smith, 'a nation of shopkeepers', and such people loved money above all things. Interference with trade could hurt two ways – what would happen to shopkeepers who had no customers? He issued a series of decrees, some from Berlin in 1806 and the others from Milan in 1807, forbidding any of his subjects and allies to trade with Britain. He hoped that British merchants would start losing money heavily, and complain hard enough to make their government ask for peace. Meanwhile the people of Europe would just have to go short of such things as sugar,

In 1808 Ackermann's 'Microcosm of London' was published, a collection of views of the most notable places in the metropolis. This is the custom house beside the Thames, one of the most important buildings in the life of what was then the greatest port in the world.

The Spanish royal family, painted in 1800 by Goya. He was the principal court painter, but this did not prevent him from showing them in a sharply un-complimentary way.

tea, coffee, tobacco and cotton. Napoleon's plan was called the Continental System.

Undoubtedly British merchants were hard hit. To make their plight worse, daring privateers darted out of French ports and captured great numbers of merchant ships. There were many bankruptcies. Some merchants, however, made money by smuggling goods from such islands as Corfu and Heligoland, which the Royal Navy had seized. Most Europeans, it seems, had no wish to go without, and they bought smuggled goods when they could.

One wide gap existed in the Continental System. The Portuguese government refused to close its ports to British ships. Napoleon could not possibly permit this. He sent an army to compel obedience. The Portuguese royal family fled under British protection to Brazil, and the French occupied Portugal.

This created a slight problem. It was necessary to cross Spain to reach Portugal. Napoleon despised the Spanish government, which had always given in to his demands but was corrupt and untrustworthy. He decided to take charge, which would not only serve his purpose in Portugal but also give the Spanish people a fairer and more efficient government. First he sent in 100,000 men, ostensibly to protect the coast against British raids. Next, politely but treacherously, he kidnapped the Spanish royal family and compelled them to abdicate. Then he appointed his brother Joseph King of Spain.

Spain exploded in his face.

Napoleon had misjudged the Spaniards. They felt insulted and they would not accept the humiliation. Spanish troops and volunteers everywhere turned on the French, who had to retire into the north of Spain. But soon reinforcements arrived. The Spanish army, badly trained and incompetently led, lost every battle, and soon the French army's position had been restored. But the war went on! The ordinary people kept it going. It cost the French army two sieges of two months each and 60,000 casualties to subdue the city of Saragossa. Peasants murdered any French soldiers they found alone or in small groups. In the hills, bands of armed men gathered, ready to pounce on small convoys and garrisons. This war without pitched battles was called *guerrilla*, or little war, but there was nothing little about the toll of death and suffering on both sides.

Goya painted this pair of pictures in 1814 to express his feelings about the beginning of the Spanish uprising in 1808. They are simply called 'The Second of May' and 'The Third of May': on one day some of the people of Madrid attacked some of Napoleon's troops — Mamelukes in this picture — and on the next the French inflicted punishment.

Sooner or later Napoleon's army might have crushed the Spaniards. A great number of troops spread widely in garrisons and mobile columns might hold down the country and hunt out the *guerrilleros*. But this was something that they were not allowed to do. Britain had an army as well as a navy, and now was the opportunity to use it.

In the summer of 1808 a force under Sir Arthur Wellesley landed in Portugal, and later that year Sir John Moore led the army into northern Spain. Though Moore was chased out, being killed by a cannonball as his army was getting aboard the ships at Corunna, Wellesley, once again commanding in Portugal, was very successful. Even when forced back by superior forces, Wellesley rested secure behind the massive defensive works of Torres Vedras which he had prepared around Lisbon, with friendly ships keeping the sea behind him. His highly trained army proved well able to beat reasonably equal numbers of French troops, and while the French were trying to overwhelm him they could not use their strength against the guerrilla bands.

This print of the Battle of Busaco, 1810, based on a contemporary soldier's sketch, shows how Wellesley preferred to fight the French. His troops would wait in line near the crest of a hill, where they could sometimes shelter from cannon fire. The French would attack in massive columns which, however, could not use their muskets nearly as effectively as well-trained infantry standing in lines. When the attack wavered, the defenders could charge down with the bayonet.

Napoleon, too busy to return to take charge in Spain himself, thought it of secondary importance. But the war, known to English-speaking historians as the Peninsular War, went on and on, and Napoleon's marshals never managed the knockout blows that their master expected them to deliver. Much later Napoleon was to refer to this war as the 'Spanish ulcer' which drained away much of the strength of his armies.

Maintaining mastery

The years 1809 to 1812 saw Napoleon at the height of his power. What opposition there was merely seemed to show how mighty he was.

In 1809, encouraged by the Peninsular War, Austria once more took up arms. This time there was a new factor. Revolts were attempted all over the German states. The people were urged to rise not because some king said so; not because the French were godless revolutionaries; not even because Napoleon was taking money and young men. The reason simply was that the French were French, and members of the German nation should not submit to foreigners. This was the cult of nationalism, which German poets and song writers were beginning to preach: devotion not so much to church or king or class or political party, but first and foremost to the nation. It was summed up in a famous song written a few years later: 'Deutschland über Alles' – Germany above everything.

As yet, however, this feeling was not strong enough to make Germany another Spain, and the revolts were quickly put down, mainly by German troops. Napoleon himself dealt with Austria. He occupied Vienna and on 29 May 1809 attacked the Austrian army at Aspern-Essling, just to the north. He had a rude shock, for the Austrians repulsed him in the nearest thing to an outright defeat that he had ever experienced in a pitched

One of the most spectacular German risings of 1809 was in the Tyrol, which Napoleon had transferred from Austria to his ally, Bavaria. The rising was led by the inn-keeper Andreas Hofer, seen here directing an attack on a castle held by the Bavarians. After many victories, the Tyrolese had to submit when Austria made peace and Napoleon could turn overwhelming force against them. Hofer was captured and shot. This print was made later in the nineteenth century, and reveals the dramatic feeling of romantic patriotism which was a powerful motive in many European political movements from 1809 onwards.

left: *Perhaps the culminating moment for Napoleon's ambitions? This painting by G. Rouget shows him presenting his son and heir to the greatest officials of his empire, the proud mother being the daughter of the Austrian emperor.*

battle. But he took his revenge at Wagram on 6 July, and once again Austria was forced to sue for peace.

This time Napoleon was not content to take only lands. He took one of the Austrian Emperor's daughters, Marie-Louise, as his wife after divorcing Josephine, his first wife. Now indeed the House of Bonaparte had forced its way into European royalty. Could there be clearer proof that Napoleon was master of Europe?

At about the same time, he extended the territories ruled directly from Paris, and the French Empire grew to its greatest size.

By these signs Napoleon was stronger than ever. It may be, though, that the growth of his empire was a sign of weakness, for he thought it necessary to rule those lands personally in order to stop the British smuggling. Even his brother Louis, whom he had made King of Holland, had abdicated rather than enforce the Continental System which was harming his subjects' trade. Napoleon may have had more power than ever, but he was being compelled to exert it. And still the Peninsular War went on.

In the east of Europe Napoleon had to rely on the friendship of the Tsar, and Alexander was ceasing to be a docile pupil. He was beginning to feel disillusioned, especially when, after Wagram, Napoleon had not given Russia a share of the Polish lands taken from Austria but had added them to the Grand Duchy of Warsaw. The Tsar began to make trouble about the enforcement of the Continental System. It became clear that if Napoleon wanted obedience he would have to enforce it. Since he now was able to put into the field more soldiers than ever before, he was very willing to teach the Tsar, once and for all, who was master of Europe. With his Grand Army of more than half a million French, Dutch, Swiss, Germans and Italians, with an allied Austrian army to the south and an allied Prussian army to the north, he invaded Russia in the summer of 1812.

Collapse

The retreat from Moscow is one of the best-known horror stories in history. We all know of the agony and death of the Grand Army in the terrible Russian winter. But Napoleon had lost before the first snowflakes fell. It was not the cold but the sheer enormity of Russia that defeated him, and the obstinate opposition of the Tsar and the Russian people. No matter how deep he thrust, there were always endless spaces ahead into which the Russians could retire, and when he tried to 'live off the country' the people destroyed all food and shelter, though this could mean death to themselves. When he saw how great the disaster was, Napoleon deserted his doomed army and fled to Paris. From here he called up more conscripts to build new armies.

1812 was the turning point. There could be no concealing a catastrophe of this size, and all those who wanted to throw off Napoleon's mastery saw that they could never hope for a better

chance. Sweden, advised by Bernadotte, a former French Marshal who had been adopted by the Swedish king as his heir, had already shown support for Britain and then Russia. Now Prussia and Austria seized the chance to change sides and join the Russians who were slowly pursuing the French westwards. The 'shopkeepers' inevitably were ready to help any enemy of Napoleon with money and arms, as they had done so often; in 1813 Britain supplied her allies with £11,000,000 and 1,000,000 muskets.

1813 was the year of decision. Germany was the battlefield. The French very nearly won again. It is sometimes forgotten that even if Napoleon's armies were now full of raw recruits, the allies were hardly better off. Russian losses in 1812 had not been so very much less than the Grand Army's, while many of the thousands of Germans who joined in what is known as the War of Liberation had more enthusiasm than training and experience. Napoleon still had such strength that at one stage his opponents agreed to attack only those French armies commanded by Marshals, never the Emperor himself. But at last the weight of numbers shifted, and Napoleon's army was over-

What the struggle against Napoleon cost the British taxpayer

whelmed in what has been called 'the battle of the nations' at Leipzig, 16–19 October. After that Napoleon withdrew across the Rhine.

In 1814, after Napoleon had rejected peace offers which would have left him holding everything west of the Rhine, the allies invaded France. Now Napoleon fought one of his most brilliant campaigns. Time and again he fell on separate parts of the allied armies and sent them reeling back. But even as he did it, the others pressed on with grim resolution, and at last took Paris. His own Marshals would fight no longer, and forced Napoleon to abdicate on 11 April.

The allies wanted to get things back to what they considered normal – if there was such a thing as 'normal' after all that had gone on since 1789. They placed on the French throne Louis XVIII, brother of Louis XVI. (The missing XVII was a boy who had died in prison during the revolution.) Napoleon was given the small Italian island of Elba as an independent kingdom, and then the leading statesmen of Europe gathered at a congress in Vienna to work out a full settlement.

There was to be one more adventure in the Napoleonic epic.

The former master of Europe could not be content with 90 square miles. When he heard that in France the returned royalists were making themselves unpopular and that in Vienna the allies were quarrelling, he took his chance. On 1 March 1815 he slipped away from Elba and landed in France with 1,000 men. On the 20th he was in Paris, Emperor once more, for his old soldiers had welcomed him. But on 18 June he met the nearest allied armies, led by the Prussian Blücher and the British Wellesley – now Duke of Wellington, at Waterloo, and his 'Hundred Days' ended in total disaster.

For Napoleon there remained six years of captivity on the lonely British island of St Helena in the South Atlantic. To those who shared his exile or came to visit him he often talked about his career, and he talked as if all he had ever really wanted was the peace and happiness of the French people. It is unlikely that he believed this himself, but many people did. Deliberately he created a picture of himself as a hero, great and good, whose fall was a tragedy for France and all Europe. Napoleon's final success was the creation of the Napoleonic Legend.

'The Last Vision', by H. Farré. This evocation of the hero's deathbed was painted in the nineteenth century and was still being sold as a postcard in the middle of the twentieth century. It tells us part of the emotions behind the Napoleonic Legend.

6 BACK TO THE OLD REGIME

The map tells what the statesmen settled at Vienna, but cannot fully explain why.

First they had to deal with France, the country which had caused all the trouble. Even after the Hundred Days most of the statesmen showed little desire for vengeance. France kept her frontiers of 1790; she only had to give up 700,000,000 francs, to help the allies with their war expenses. This mildness was partly because the Vienna statesmen wanted the French to settle down quietly under the king without any reason to feel aggrieved, partly because a severe weakening of France would have upset any Balance of Power. However, some precautions had to be taken; allied garrisons occupied some French fortresses for a few years, and some of France's neighbours were strengthened, as in the Netherlands and Northern Italy.

The allies, of course, wanted to give themselves rewards, and there were bitter disputes. On the whole, however, they shared out the spoils cleverly, keeping the balance fairly even.

On one thing all were agreed: the rightful royal families must be restored to their thrones. Many believed in the principle of *legitimacy*. This was that no power could ever stop the lawful king from being king; even if he were killed, there would be a legitimate successor somewhere. This may sound similar to the old Divine Right theory, but there was a practical reason why it became so popular now. Unless the legitimate king were accepted as the highest authority in a state, it was difficult to produce a very convincing argument that the people were not the sovereign power. Royalty seemed the only sound defence against revolution.

Common sense, however, forbade a total return to 1789. For example, the Holy Roman Empire had been such a sham that nobody could seriously suggest restoring it. So a new Germanic Confederation was set up, with the Austrian Emperor as president, and including only thirty-nine member states instead of nearly ten times that number. (Smaller princes kept their lands, but each within a larger state.) Still this was too much like the old Empire to be anything but a bitter disappointment to any German who had fought not only to get rid of the French but for a united nation or, at least, a federal state.

The Poles were another disappointed nation. Napoleon had partly restored their country as a Grand Duchy. Now, though Poland regained the rank of Kingdom, it was given the Tsar as king. It was not that the Vienna statesmen dreaded nationalism as they did 'Jacobinism', but they did not rate it very highly, and the claims of legitimate monarchs must come first.

They foresaw that after such upheavals and such elaborate treaties there would be difficulties and disputes. Europe needed tranquillity. There must be no trouble between the big powers. Therefore the leaders at Vienna agreed to hold further congresses from time to time so that they could try to solve any problems which might disturb the peace of Europe. The Tsar, still something of an idealist, proposed a Holy Alliance in which rulers agreed to behave like Christians towards one another and towards their subjects; most signed. In their different ways the Congress System and the Holy Alliance showed the great powers trying to devise some sort of international plan to avert wars. It had never been attempted before, and was a fine idea.

There were thousands of people in Europe, some who had come to believe in liberty after the successes of the revolutionaries, some who had put their faith in nationalism, who looked at it very differently. They saw the Holy Alliance as a conspiracy to crush liberty and to prevent nations from governing themselves. It is possible for us to understand their feelings. But it is also possible, looking back, to recognize in the men of Vienna people who had been brought up in the civilization of the eighteenth century and who were trying to restore and protect the values of that civilization. They were trying to continue the eighteenth century into the nineteenth, across the revolution that lay between.

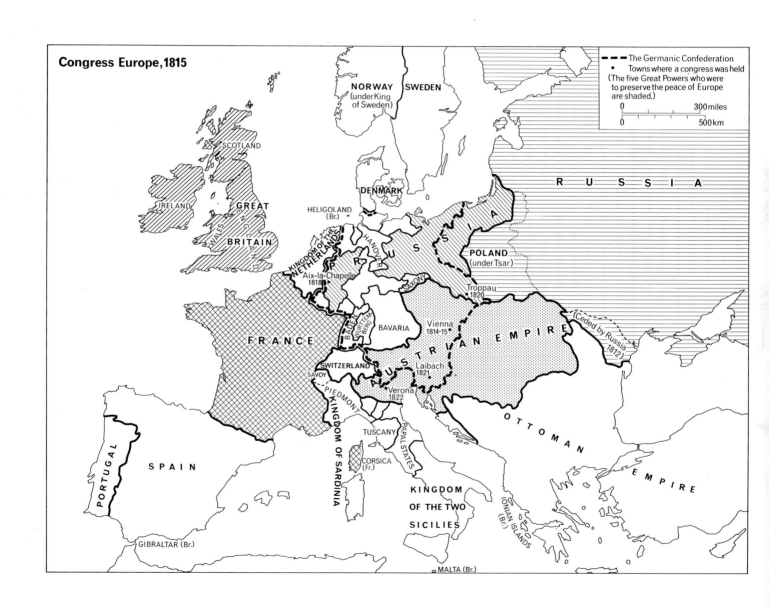

Congress Europe, 1815

- - - The Germanic Confederation
• Towns where a congress was held
(The five Great Powers who were
to preserve the peace of Europe
are shaded.)

0   300miles
0   500km

NORWAY SWEDEN
(under King
of Sweden)

R U S S I A

SCOTLAND

IRELAND GREAT

WALES BRITAIN

DENMARK

HELIGOLAND
(Br.)

KINGDOM OF THE
NETHERLANDS

HANOVER

P R U S S I A

POLAND
(under Tsar)

Aix-la-Chapelle
1818

SAXONY

Troppau
1820

BADEN

WÜRTEM-
BERG

BAVARIA

Vienna
1814-15

A U S T R I A N E M P I R E

(Ceded by Russia
1812)

FRANCE

SWITZERLAND

SAVOY

Laibach
1821

PIEDMONT

Verona
1822

PORTUGAL

SPAIN

KINGDOM OF SARDINIA

TUSCANY

PAPAL STATES

CORSICA
(Fr.)

O T T O M A N

E M P I R E

KINGDOM

OF THE TWO

SICILIES

(IONIAN ISLANDS
(Br.)

GIBRALTAR (Br.)

MALTA (Br.)

Index

Acknowledgments

Illustrations in this volume are reproduced by kind permission of the following:
Front cover, 5, 8, 69 (Mme Roland) Musée de Versailles, clichés des Musées Nationaux, Paris; pp. 4, 7, 22, 24, 32, 64, 68, 75, 82 Photographie Giraudon; pp. 6, 7, 10, 39, 63, 66, 72, 74 Bibliothèque Nationale; p. 15 Rijksmuseum, Amsterdam; pp. 18, 20 (Hanover Square), 25, 27, 58, 65, 78, 90, 91, 96 British Museum; p. 18 (bust by Rastrelli) Novosti Press Agency; p. 20 J. E. Dayton; p. 20 (Castletown) Irish Tourist Board; p. 21 Kunsthistorisches Museum, Vienna; p. 23 Fitzwilliam Museum, Cambridge; p. 28 Tate Gallery, London; p. 29 Sir John Soane's Museum; pp. 30, 35, 39 (Pugachev), 50, 53, 55, 69, 83 (Café Frascati), 87 Cambridge University Library; pp. 31 (balloon), 46, 47, 63 (Tennis Court), 71, 72 (cartoon), 79, 83 Mansell Collection; p. 31 Science Museum, London; p. 32 (Voltaire) Victoria and Albert Museum; p. 33 National Gallery of Scotland; p. 34 Castle Howard Collection, York, England; p. 37 Bildarchiv Preussischer Kulturbesitz; p. 41 Graphischen Sammlung Albertina, photo Lichtbildwerkstätte Alpenland; pp. 43, 45 Director of the India Office Library and Records; pp. 48, 49 Colonial Williamsburg Foundation; p. 52 Library of Congress; p. 56 Connecticut Historical Society; p. 57 Yale University Art Gallery; p. 60 New York Public Library; p. 61 Museum of the City of New York; pp. 62, 68 (assignat), 70 Photographie Bulloz; p. 67 Bowes Museum, Durham; pp. 75 (Napoleon), 91 (Napoleon) Photo Hachette; p. 76 National Maritime Museum, London; p. 77 Duke of Wellington, Stratfield Saye House Collection; pp. 80, 96 (Congress of Vienna) by gracious permission of Her Majesty Queen Elizabeth II; pp. 81, 88, 89, back cover, Museo del Prado; p. 93 Les Editions Nomis, Paris.

Maps and diagrams by
Reg Piggott and Leslie Marshall

Front cover: *In the Sun King's palace at Versailles there is a salon decorated in honour of Apollo, god of the sun. This emblem appears on the carved and gilded doors.*

Back cover: *In a park near Madrid, ladies and gentlemen have assembled to admire the latest ingenious device from France, a Montgolfier hot-air balloon. Painting by Antonio Carnicero, 1748–1801.*

The Cambridge History Library

The Cambridge Introduction to History
Written by Trevor Cairns

The Cambridge Topic Books
General Editor Trevor Cairns

The Cambridge History Library will be expanded in the future to include additional volumes. Lerner Publications Company is pleased to participate in making this excellent series of books available to a wide audience of readers.